THE TEENS' WORKBOOK TO SELF REGULATE ADVANCED EDITION

*Mastering Emotional Intelligence
Through Advanced CBT Techniques
and Resilience Building*

Richard Bass

2 FREE Bonuses!

Receive a **FREE** Planner for Kids and a copy of the Positive Discipline Playbook by scanning below!

Contents

Conclusion:

About the Author

References

Introduction

The greatest discovery of all time is that a person can change their future by merely changing their attitude.

- Oprah Winfrey

Welcome back to your journey of emotional growth and self-discovery! If you've completed The Teens' Workbook to Self-Regulate, you've already built a strong foundation in understanding your emotions, thoughts, and behaviors. This advanced workbook will take you even further, helping you develop sophisticated skills for managing complex emotional situations and building lasting resilience.

Recent studies show that teenagers who develop advanced emotional regulation skills are better equipped to handle future challenges, maintain healthy relationships, and achieve their goals. According to the American Psychological Association's 2023 report on teen mental health, adolescents who master advanced coping strategies show significant improvements in academic performance, social relationships, and overall well-being.

This workbook introduces advanced concepts and techniques through 36 new exercises, building upon the skills you've already learned. You'll explore:

- *Deep-seated patterns of thinking and behavior (schemas)*
- *Advanced awareness of your thought processes (metacognition)*
- *Sophisticated emotional regulation techniques*
- *Complex social intelligence skills*
- *Lifestyle integration strategies*
- *Future planning tools*

Additionally, you'll find bonus materials including a 14 day self regulation plan, in which you will apply what you've learned in this workbook to real-life situations. Each day, you'll focus on a specific self-regulation skill through simple but effective exercise. By the end of these 14 days, you'll have a stronger ability to manage emotions, navigate social situations, and plan for your future.

How to Use This Advanced Workbook

1. **Progressive Learning:** While exercises build upon basic concepts, each section begins with a clear explanation of new advanced concepts you'll be working with.
2. **Personalized Pace:** Take your time with each exercise. Some advanced concepts might require more reflection and practice.
3. **Integration Focus:** Each chapter includes specific strategies for integrating new skills into your daily life.
4. **Support System:** Consider sharing your progress with a trusted adult, counselor, or mentor who can support your journey.
5. **Practical Application:** Look for the "Real-Life Application" boxes throughout the workbook that provide concrete examples of how to use these advanced skills in everyday situations.

What's Different in This Advanced Workbook?

- More complex scenarios and solutions
- Deeper exploration of thought patterns
- Advanced emotional regulation techniques
- Integration of multiple skills
- Long-term planning and sustainability focus
- System-based approaches to emotional management

Remember, this workbook is designed to challenge you while providing the support and guidance you need to succeed. Your commitment to personal growth is admirable, and each exercise you complete is a step toward becoming more emotionally resilient and self-aware.

Are you ready to take your emotional regulation skills to the next level? Let's begin with Chapter 1, where we'll explore the powerful world of schemas and how they shape your experiences.

Schema Work

"Your beliefs become your thoughts, your thoughts become your words, your words become your actions, your actions become your habits, your habits become your values, your values become your destiny."

- Mahatma Gandhi

Understanding Advanced Schemas

What if you could understand the deep patterns that guide your reactions and behaviors? That's exactly what schemas help us discover. Schemas are like the "operating system" of your mind - they're deep-seated patterns of thinking and behaving that developed early in your life and continue to influence how you see yourself, others, and the world.

What Are Schemas?

Schemas are like invisible lenses through which you view life. They develop based on your early experiences and can affect:

- *How you view yourself*
- *What you expect from others*
- *How you react to situations*
- *What you believe is possible for your future*

Real-Life Application:

Sarah always felt she had to be perfect to be loved. This was her "Unrelenting Standards" schema. When she got a B on a test, she'd think "I'm not good enough" and study until midnight. Understanding this schema helped her realize she was worthy of love regardless of her grades.

Common Teen Schemas

- *1. Abandonment: Fear that important people in your life will leave*
- *2. Defectiveness: Feeling fundamentally flawed or unlovable*
- *3. Dependence: Believing you can't handle things on your own*
- *4. Unrelenting Standards: Feeling you must be perfect*
- *5. Entitlement: Believing you deserve special treatment*
- *6. Social Isolation: Feeling different or not belonging*

Let's explore these patterns through six powerful exercises that will help you understand and work with your schemas.

Schema Detective Work

Purpose:

To become a skilled detective of your own thought patterns, like a CSI investigator uncovering clues about how your past experiences shape your current reactions. Just as detectives gather evidence to solve cases, you'll collect evidence about your schemas (deep patterns of thinking and behaving) to better understand yourself.

Materials Needed:

- Pen or pencil
- Quiet space for reflection
- Open and curious mindset

Real-Life Application:

Maya always felt she had to be perfect at everything or she was worthless (Unrelenting Standards schema). When she got a B+ on a test, she'd spiral into negative thoughts and stay up all night studying. After doing schema detective work, she discovered this pattern started when she was young and got praised only for perfect grades. Understanding this helped her realize she was worthy regardless of grades and could work on building a more balanced view of success.

Step 1: Initial Schema Investigation

Rate how much each schema statement feels true for you (0 = Not at all true, 5 = Completely true). Think of this like gathering your first set of clues:

Schemas about Self-Worth:

- "I must be perfect to be acceptable":

- "I'm fundamentally flawed or defective":

- "I'm not as good as other people":

Schemas about Relationships:

- "People will eventually abandon me":

- "I can't trust others to be there for me":

- "I must please others to be accepted":

Schemas about Competence:

- "I can't handle things on my own":

- "I must always be in control":

- "I'm going to fail no matter what":

Pro Tip: *Be honest with yourself - these are just clues to help you understand your patterns, not judgments about who you are.*

Step 2: Schema Story Investigation

For your highest-rated schema from Step 1, think of a recent situation where this pattern appeared. Like a detective reconstructing a scene, capture all the details:

The Setting:

- *When did it happen?* _____
- *Where were you?* _____
- *Who was involved?* _____
- *What triggered it?* _____

Your Internal Experience:

- *First thoughts:* _____
- *Emotions felt:* _____
- *Body sensations:* _____
- *Automatic reactions:* _____

Your Actions:

- *What you did:* _____
- *How others responded:* _____
- *What happened next:* _____
- *How it ended:* _____

Pro Tip: *Try to be as specific as possible - small details often provide the biggest insights!*

Step 3: Schema Pattern Analysis

Looking at your story from Step 2, let's analyze the pattern like a detective finding connections:

Pattern Recognition:

- *How often does this happen?*_____
- *In what situations?*_____
- *With which people?*_____
- *What usually triggers it?*_____

Impact Assessment:

- How does it affect your:
  - *Relationships?*_____
  - *School/work?*_____
  - *Self-image?*_____
  - *Daily life?*_____

Origin Investigation:

- *When did you first notice this pattern?*_____
- *What was happening in your life then?*_____
- *Who influenced this belief?*_____
- *What kept it going?*_____

Step 4: Evidence Collection

Like a detective gathering proof, collect evidence that challenges your schema:

Evidence Against The Schema:

- 1. Times when the opposite was true:_____
- 2. People who see you differently: _____
- 3. Achievements that disprove it:_____
- 4. Positive feedback you've received:_____

Alternative Explanations:

- 1. Other ways to view the situation: _____
- 2. What you'd tell a friend: _____
- 3. A balanced perspective: _____

Pro Tip: Keep this evidence handy for when your schema gets triggered - it's like having fact-checking tools ready!

Step 5: Create Your Schema Support System

Build your support team like a detective's network of trusted contacts:

Support People:

- Who can help challenge this pattern?_____
- Who sees your true value?_____
- Who can offer perspective?_____

Coping Strategies:

- What helps when triggered?_____

- How can you self-soothe?_____

- What reminds you of your worth?_____

Step 6: Design Your Schema Growth Plan

Create your action plan like a detective's case strategy:

Daily Practices:

- **1. Morning reminder:** _____
  Example: "Today, I will be patient with myself and open to learning."

- **2. Self-check moments:** _____
  Example: "Before reacting, I'll ask: Is this thought helping me or holding me back?"

- **3. Evening reflection:** _____
  Example: "What's one small win I had today, even if it was just trying?"

Weekly Goals:

- **1. Skills to practice:** _____
  Example: "Practice pausing before responding when I feel frustrated."

- **2. Support to seek:** _____
  Example: "Ask a friend how they handle stressful situations."

- **3. Challenges to try:** _____
  Example: "Go a full day without negative self-talk–replace each one with a neutral or positive thought."

Monthly Review:

- **1. Progress notes:** _____
  Example: "I noticed I get less frustrated when I pause before reacting."

- **2. Pattern changes:** _____
  Example: "I'm catching my unhelpful thoughts quicker and replacing them."

○ **3. Next steps:**_____
　　　<u>Example:</u> *"Try expressing my emotions calmly in tough conversations."*

<u>Pro Tips for Schema Detective Success</u>:
- ○ *Start with the schema that impacts you most*
- ○ *Keep detailed notes of your investigations*
- ○ *Look for patterns across different situations*
- ○ *Be patient - understanding takes time*
- ○ *Celebrate small insights and progress*
- ○ *Share discoveries with trusted supporters*
- ○ *Remember: awareness leads to change*

<u>Remember:</u> *Just like a detective solving a case, understanding your schemas takes time and patience. Each insight is a clue leading you toward better self-understanding!*

Progress Tracking:

<u>*Example:*</u>
Week 1
- Rate your schema awareness (1-10): **6**

Key Insight:
- *I tend to oversimplify schemas in some contexts and need to better understand the nuances of how they influence behavior.*

Next Focus:
- *Deepen my understanding of schema theory by identifying examples of my own core schemas in daily interactions.*

Week 1

- Rate your schema awareness (1-10):

Key Insight:

_____

_____

Next Focus:

_____

_____

Week 2

- *Rate your schema awareness (1-10):*

Key Insight:

_____

_____

Next Focus:

_____

_____

Week 3

- *Rate your schema awareness (1-10):*

Key Insight:

_____

_____

Next Focus:

_____

_____

Week 4

- *Rate your schema awareness (1-10):*

Key Insight:

_____

_____

Next Focus:

_____

_____

Schema Story Rewrite

Purpose:

To become the author of your own life story by learning how to recognize and rewrite the narratives your schemas create. Think of yourself as a movie director who can yell "CUT!" and reshoot a scene from a different angle, or a writer who can revise a story to create a better ending.

Materials Needed:

- Pen or pencil
- Your favorite writing spot
- Open mind for new perspectives
- Schema insights from Exercise 43

Real-Life Application Example:

Jordan always interpreted silence in group conversations as "Everyone hates me and thinks I'm stupid" *(Defectiveness/Social Exclusion schema)*. During a class project, when teammates were quietly thinking after his idea, he almost withdrew completely. But using story rewriting skills, he caught his schema's interpretation and rewrote it: "People are thoughtfully considering my idea. Silence can mean thinking, not rejection." This new story helped him stay engaged, and eventually, his teammates built on his idea to create their best project yet!

Step 1: Story Collection

A. Identify Your Schema Stories

Choose three recent situations where your schema showed up. Like a journalist gathering stories, capture the details:

Story 1 Example:

- **What happened?** *My friend didn't reply to my text for two days.*
- **How your schema interpreted it:** *They must not like me anymore.*
- **Emotions felt:** *Sad, rejected.*
- **Actions taken:** *Ignored their next message.*
- **Impact on outcome:** *Our friendship felt awkward for a while.*

Now it is your turn fill out the template below:

Story 1:

- **What happened?**_____
- **How your schema interpreted it:**_____
- **Emotions felt:**_____
- **Actions taken:**_____
- **Impact on outcome:**_____

Story 2:

- **What happened?**_____
- **How your schema interpreted it:**_____
- **Emotions felt:**_____
- **Actions taken:**_____
- **Impact on outcome:** _____

Story 3:

- **What happened?**_____
- **How your schema interpreted it:**_____
- **Emotions felt:**_____
- **Actions taken:**_____
- **Impact on outcome:**_____

Step 2: Story Analysis

Like an editor reviewing a manuscript, examine each story's elements.

Schema Pattern Detection Example:

- **What triggered the schema?** *Seeing someone not reply to me.*
- **What assumptions were made?** *They must be mad at me.*
- **What "rules" did your schema follow?** *If someone doesn't respond fast, it means I'm not important.*
- **What predictions did it make?** *They won't want to talk to me anymore.*
- **How did these affect your actions?** *I ignored their message instead of clarifying.*

Now it is your turn fill out the template below:

Schema Pattern Detection:

- **What triggered the schema?**_____
- **What assumptions were made?**_____
- **What "rules" did your schema follow?**_____
- **What predictions did it make?**_____
- **How did these affect your actions?**_____

- **If a friend told you this story, what would you say?** _Maybe they were busy and couldn't reply right away._
- **If you were feeling confident, how would you see it?** _It's okay–they'll reply when they have time._
- **If your schema wasn't active, what might you notice?** _They've always been kind to me; one slow reply doesn't change that._

Now it is your turn fill out the template below:

Schema Pattern Detection:

- **If a friend told you this story, what would you say?** _____

  _____

- **If you were feeling confident, how would you see it?** _____

  _____

- **If your schema wasn't active, what might you notice?** _____

  _____

Step 3: Story Rewriting Workshop

Original Schema Version Example:

- **Setting:** _At school._
- **Characters involved:** _Classmates._
- **Schema's interpretation:** _Everyone thinks I'm weird because I answered the question wrong._
- **Emotional tone:** _Embarrassed and nervous._
- **Ending:** _I avoided raising my hand again._

Alternative Version 1 (Balanced Perspective) Example:

- **New interpretation:** *It's okay to make mistakes; everyone does.*
- **Evidence supporting this view:** *Another classmate made a mistake earlier, and nobody laughed.*
- **Different emotions possible:** *Relief, acceptance.*
- **Alternative actions available:** *Raise my hand again to try.*
- **Potential different outcome:** *I participate more and learn better.*

Alternate Version 1 (Balance Perspective)

- **Setting:**_____
- **Characters involved:**_____
- **Schema's interpretation:**_____
- **Emotional tone:**_____
- **Ending:**_____

Alternative Version 2 (Best Case)

- **Setting:**_____
- **Characters involved:**_____
- **Schema's interpretation:**_____
- **Emotional tone:**_____
- **Ending:**_____

Alternative Version 3 (Realistic Middle)

- Setting:_____
- Characters involved:_____
- Schema's interpretation:_____
- Emotional tone:_____
- Ending:_____

Step 4: Story Testing Laboratory

Small Test Scenario Example:

- **Safe situation to try:** _Reply to my friend's message after a delay._
- **New story to practice:** _"They're busy, not ignoring me."_
- **What success looks like:** _Feeling calm and keeping the conversation going._
- **Support needed:** _Reminder from a family member._
- **Backup plan if triggered:** _Pause and breathe before replying._

Now it is your turn fill out the template below:

Schema Pattern Detection:

- **Safe situation to try:**_____
- **New story to practice:**_____
- **What success looks like:**_____
- **Support needed:**_____
- **Backup plan if triggered:**_____

Repeat for Medium Challenge Scenario and Full Challenge Scenario.

Step 5: Story Integration Strategies

Like a director rehearsing scenes, practice integrating your new stories into daily life.

Daily Practice Plan

Morning review: *Choose one new story to focus on for the day.*

_____

_____

_____

_____

_____

_____

_____

<u>**Example:**</u> *"Today, I'll remind myself that quiet moments during group discussions mean reflection, not rejection."*

Situation check-ins:

Pause during situations where your schema is triggered. Ask, "What story am I telling myself right now?" _____

_____

_____

Evening reflection:

Write about your successes and challenges in using your new stories.

_____

_____

_____

_____

_____

_____

_____

_____

Quick Rewrite Tools

Keep these prompts handy to shift your perspective quickly:

Schema spotting phrases: _"Am I assuming the worst again?"_

_____

_____

Example: _"Am I assuming they don't like me because of a facial expression?"_

Reality check questions: *"What else could be true?"*

_____

_____

_____

Perspective shift prompts: *"What would my confident self think?"*

_____

_____

_____

_____

Evidence gathering cues: *"What facts support this new story?"*

_____

_____

_____

_____

Support system signals: *"Who can I talk to for reassurance?"*

_____

_____

_____

_____

Story Strengthening Exercises
Write your new story daily.

_____

_____

_____

Example: *"During group work, people respect my ideas."*

Share your story with a support person.

_____

_____

Practice in low-stress moments.
Example: *"I'll try rewriting my interpretation of non-verbal signals during dinner."*

_____

_____

_____

_____

How will you celebrate small successes.

_____

_____

_____

_____

How will you learn from setbacks.

_____

_____

_____

_____

Step 6: Create Your Rewriting Success Kit

Build a personal toolkit for ongoing story rewriting success.

Schema Story Spotting Tools

Keep these prompts handy to shift your perspective quickly:

Physical signals: *Notice body tension, rapid heartbeat, or other stress signals. What signals do you notice?*

_____

_____

_____

Emotional flags: *Watch for strong feelings like shame, fear, or anger.*

When I feel _____, my _____ schema is active.

Thought patterns: *Spot negative self-talk or assumptions, and write them below.*

_____

_____

_____

Behavior alerts: Note when you withdraw, lash out, or people-please.

Example: *"I wanted to avoid the group after they didn't immediately respond."*

_____

_____

_____

Quick Rewrite Scripts

When I notice [schema thought] _____ **, I'll say:**

_____

_____

_____

Example: *"When I think 'They don't care about my ideas,' I'll say, 'They need time to think about it.'"*

When I feel [schema emotion] _____ **, I'll remember:**

_____

_____

_____

When I start to [schema behavior] _____ **,I'll try:**

_____

_____

_____

Emergency Rewrite Kit

Keep these handy for intense schema moments:

Power statements: _____

_____

_____

 Example: "Silence doesn't equal rejection. It's okay to wait."

Evidence cards: _Write down facts that challenge your schema's assumptions._

_____

_____

Support contacts: _List people who can help you rewrite your story._

_____

_____

_____

Coping strategies: _Practice breathing exercises, take a walk, or journal._

_____

_____

_____

Success reminders: _Keep a list of times you successfully rewrote a schema story._

_____

_____

Step 7: Track Your Rewriting Progress

Document your story transformation journey and measure growth.

Weekly Check-in

Stories rewritten:_____

Challenges faced:_____

Lessons learned:_____

Monthly Review

Skills improved:_____

Example: *"I'm better at recognizing when my schema is triggered."*

Patterns changed:_____

Relationships affected:_____

New strengths:_____

Growth areas:_____

Schema Story Scale

Rate how often you can catch and rewrite stories:

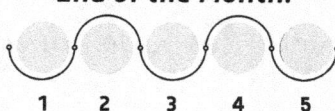

Start of the Month: 1 2 3 4 5

End of the Month: 1 2 3 4 5

Schema Challenge Ladder

Purpose:

To build your schema-challenging muscles gradually and safely, like an athlete training for a big game. Think of this as creating your personal "exposure ladder" - starting with manageable steps and working your way up to bigger challenges. Just as you wouldn't start weight training with the heaviest weights, you'll begin with smaller schema challenges and progressively build your strength.

Materials Needed:

- Pen or pencil
- Quiet space for planning
- Support person to review your ladder
- Schema insights from Exercises 43-44
- Willingness to take small steps

Real-Life Application

Alex had an Abandonment schema that made them terrified of reaching out to make new friends. Instead of forcing themselves into overwhelming social situations, they created a challenge ladder: starting with smiling at classmates (step 1), then giving compliments (step 2), making small talk (step 3), and gradually working up to initiating lunch plans (step 8). By following their ladder's steps, they built confidence at their own pace and eventually developed several close friendships!

Step 1: Choose Your Target Schema

Identify which schema you want to work on first:

☐ Abandonment *(fear of being left)*
☐ Defectiveness *(feeling fundamentally flawed)*
☐ Mistrust *(difficulty trusting others)*
☐ Social Isolation *(feeling different/not belonging)*
☐ Dependence *(feeling unable to handle things alone)*
☐ Failure *(believing you'll inevitably fail)*
☐ Unrelenting Standards *(perfectionism)*
☐ Other:_____

Rate its current impact on your life:

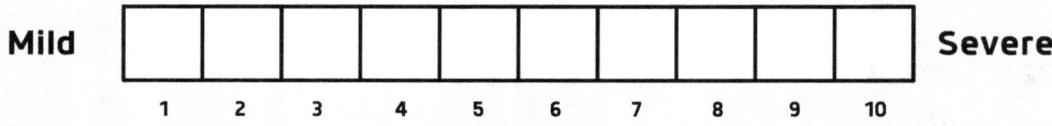

Mild
1	2	3	4	5	6	7	8	9	10
 Severe

How it affects your:

- *Relationships:*_____
- *School/Work:*_____
- *Self-image:*_____
- *Daily choices:*_____

Pro Tip: *Start with a schema that causes significant distress but doesn't feel completely overwhelming. Think "challenging but doable."*

Step 2: Build Your Challenge Ladder

Create your personal ladder with 8-10 steps, starting very small:

Step Design Template:

1. *What exactly will you do?*_____

2. *Where will you do it?*_____

3. *Who will be involved?*_____

4. *How long will it last?*_____

5. *What support will you need?*_____

6. *How will you know you succeeded?*_____

Example Ladder for Abandonment Schema:

1. *Smile at one classmate (Anxiety Level: 2/10)*
2. *Give one compliment (Anxiety Level: 3/10)*
3. *Ask a question in class (Anxiety Level: 4/10)*
4. *Make small talk before class (Anxiety Level: 5/10)*
5. *Join a study group (Anxiety Level: 6/10)*
6. *Share an opinion in group (Anxiety Level: 7/10)*
7. *Suggest a group activity (Anxiety Level: 8/10)*
8. *Make individual plans (Anxiety Level: 9/10)*

Your Personal Challenge Ladder:

Step 1 (Easiest):

- *Action:*_____
- *Anxiety Level (1-10):*_____
- *Success looks like:*_____
- *Support needed:*_____

Step 2:

- Action:_____

- Anxiety Level (1-10):_____

- Success looks like:_____

- Support needed:_____

Step 3:

- Action:_____

- Anxiety Level (1-10):_____

- Success looks like:_____

- Support needed:_____

Step 4:

- Action:_____

- Anxiety Level (1-10):_____

- Success looks like:_____

- Support needed:_____

Step 5:

- Action:_____

- Anxiety Level (1-10):_____

- Success looks like:_____

- Support needed:_____

Step 6:

- Action:_____

- Anxiety Level (1-10):_____

- Success looks like:_____

- Support needed:_____

Step 7:

- Action:_____

- Anxiety Level (1-10):_____

- Success looks like:_____

- Support needed:_____

Step 8:

- Action:_____

- Anxiety Level (1-10):_____

- Success looks like:_____

- Support needed:_____

Pro Tip: *Each step should be slightly more challenging than the last, but not so big that it feels impossible. Think baby steps!*

Step 3: Preparation Strategy for Each Step

Create a detailed plan for tackling each rung:

Pre-Challenge Checklist:

- Specific day/time chosen:————————————————————
- Location selected:—————————————————————————
- Support person notified:————————————————————
- Coping tools ready:————————————————————————
- Success criteria clear:————————————————————
- Reward planned:—————————————————————————

During Challenge Tools:

- Breathing exercise:————————————————————————
- Grounding technique:————————————————————————
- Positive self-talk phrases:————————————————————
- Reality check questions:————————————————————
- Exit strategy if needed:————————————————————

Post-Challenge Review:

- What worked well:————————————————————————
- What was difficult:————————————————————————
- What I learned:—————————————————————————
- Next time adjustments:————————————————————
- Celebration plan:————————————————————————

Step 4: Support System Setup

Build your challenge support network:

Pre-Challenge Checklist:

- Name:_____
- Role:_____
- How they'll help:_____
- Best way to contact:_____
- What to tell them:_____

Backup Support Person:

- Name: _____
- Role:_____
- How they'll help: _____
- Best way to contact:_____
- What to tell them: _____

Professional Support (if applicable):

- Name: _____
- Role: _____
- How they'll help:_____
- When to contact:_____

Step 5: Create Your Challenge Toolkit

Below are some tools to help you create your challenge toolkit.

Beginner Level Word Bank

Breathing Exercises	Grounding Techniques	Quick Statements Bank	Exit Strategy Options
• Box breathing (4-4-4-4) • Counted breaths (1-10) • Ocean breath • Mountain breath • Finger trace breathing • Balloon breath • Bubble breath • Square breath	• Temperature check • Color scan • Object focus • Sound counting • Texture touching • Movement tracking • Weather noticing • Room description	• Single word anchors • Two-word mantras • "I am" statements • Nature metaphors • Weather comparisons • Simple truths • Basic affirmations • Brief reminders	• Time-based exits • Task-based exits • Physical needs exits • Schedule references • Commitment mentions • Health-related exits • Transportation timing • Device checks

Intermediate Level Word Bank

Extended Calming Practices	Reality Check Methods	Coping Statement Themes	Backup Plan Categories
• Progressive muscle relaxation • Guided visualization • Walking meditation • Seated meditation • Energy clearing • Mental rehearsal • Quiet place imagery • Safe space creation	• Evidence listing • Past experience review • Future projection • Probability assessment • Perspective shift • Outcome analysis • Impact evaluation • Time-frame check	• Growth mindset phrases • Capability reminders • Progress acknowledgments • Strength recognition • Challenge acceptance • Change embracing • Resilience statements • Experience validation	• Social adjustments • Environmental modifications • Time management shifts • Activity alternatives • Communication options • Location changes • Group size variations • Intensity adjustments

Advanced Level Word Bank

Relaxation Routines Components	Schema Reframing Approaches	Power Phrase Themes	Recovery Strategy Elements
• Body scanning • Breath work sequences • Visualization series • Movement patterns • Sound therapy • Energy practices • Mindfulness exercises • Meditation progressions	• Core belief examination • Pattern recognition • Historical analysis • Future visioning • Value alignment • Narrative revision • Identity exploration • Belief testing	• Self-worth statements • Capability declarations • Boundary assertions • Growth celebrations • Connection affirmations • Change embracement • Resilience recognition • Agency acknowledgment	• Physical self-care • Emotional processing • Social connection • Creative expression • Nature engagement • Movement practices • Reflection methods • Celebration rituals

Additional Categories for Customization

- Time durations
- Energy levels
- Social involvement
- Physical components
- Mental engagement
- Emotional intensity
- Environmental needs
- Resource requirements

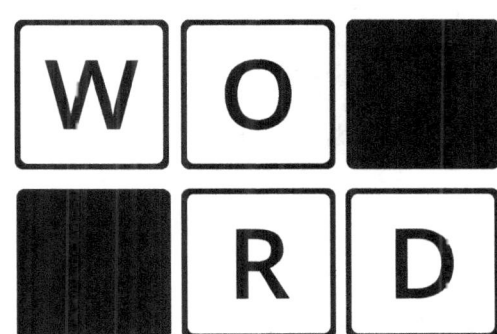

Use the word bank above to fill in your tools below:

Essential tools for each challenge level:

Beginner Level Tools (Steps 1-3):

- *Quick breathing exercise:* _____

- *Simple grounding technique:* _____

- *Basic positive statement:*_____
- *Easy exit strategy:*_____

Intermediate Level Tools (Steps 4-6):

- *Extended calming practice:*_____
- *Detailed reality checks:*_____
- *Strong coping statements:*_____
- *Backup plans:*_____

Advanced Level Tools (Steps 7-8):

- *Complete relaxation routine:*_____
- *Deep schema reframing work:*_____
- *Power phrases:*_____
- *Recovery strategies:*_____

Step 6: Progress Tracking System

Document your journey up the ladder:

Daily Practice Log:

- *Date:*_____
- *Step attempted:*_____
- *Success level (1-10):*_____
- *Key learning:*_____
- *Next attempt plan:*_____

Weekly Review:

- Steps completed:_____
- Biggest victory:_____
- Main challenge:_____
- Skill improvement:_____
- Next week's goal:_____

Monthly Progress Chart:

- Steps mastered:_____
- New skills gained:_____
- Confidence level changes:_____
- Schema strength changes:_____
- Relationship impacts:_____

Step 7: Challenge Recovery Plan

Create your bounce-back strategy:

If a step feels too hard:

1. Pause and:_____
2. Remind yourself:_____
3. Use this tool:_____
4. Contact:_____
5. Next step is:_____

If you need a break:

1. Tell yourself:_____
2. Do this activity:_____
3. For this long:_____
4. Return when:_____
5. Starting with:_____

If you want to quit:

1. Remember why you started:_____
2. Look at progress made:_____
3. Talk to:_____
4. Review successes:_____
5. Adjust plan by:_____

Pro Tips for Success:

- Stay on each step until it feels manageable
- Celebrate EVERY attempt, not just "perfect" ones
- Keep a success journal to track progress
- Share your wins with your support team
- Remember that setbacks are normal and help you learn
- Take breaks when needed but don't give up
- Focus on progress, not perfection
- Trust the process - small steps add up
- Be patient with yourself
- Each challenge makes you stronger

Schema Challenge Wisdom:

1. Tell yourself:_____

2. Do this activity:_____

3. For this long:_____

4. Return when:_____

5. Starting with:_____

Remember: Just like climbing a ladder, you can't skip steps - but each step gets you closer to your goal. Take your time, celebrate each rung, and know that every small challenge helps weaken your schema's power!

Schema Origins Map

Purpose:

To understand where your schemas (core beliefs about yourself and the world) came from and how they developed over time, like a detective tracing the history of important clues.

Materials Needed:

- Pen or pencil
- Your life timeline notes
- Quiet reflection space
- Willingness to explore past experiences

Real-Life Application

Jordan mapped his "Not Good Enough" schema back through his life experiences. He discovered it started when he was 4 and his older sibling always finished puzzles faster. It grew stronger when his first-grade teacher compared him to other students, and developed further when he didn't make the soccer team at 12. Understanding these origins helped Jordan realize his schema wasn't based on facts about his abilities, but on specific experiences that he could now view differently.

Step 1: Map Your Schema Timeline

Reflect on early experiences to understand your schema.

Use the timeline below to map key memories that shaped your schema. Follow the example provided and reflect on early events that contributed to your beliefs about yourself.

Schema being explored: Not Good Enough

- **Early Memory:** *Age 4 - Sibling solving puzzles faster*

- **How I felt:** *Frustrated, small*

- **What I concluded:** *Others are naturally better*

- **Who was involved:** *Older sibling, parents watching*

- **Environment:** *Living room after dinner*

- **Message learned:** *I'm slower, less capable*

Your Timeline Maps:

Map 1:

1. *Schema being explored:*_____

2. *Early Memory:*_____

3. *How I felt:*_____

4. *What I concluded:*_____

5. *Who was involved:*_____

6. *Environment:*_____

7. *Message learned:*_____

Map 2:

1. Schema being explored: _____

2. Early Memory: _____

3. How I felt: _____

4. What I concluded: _____

5. Who was involved: _____

6. Environment: _____

7. Message learned: _____

Map 3:

1. Schema being explored: _____

2. Early Memory: _____

3. How I felt: _____

4. What I concluded: _____

5. Who was involved: _____

6. Environment: _____

7. Message learned: _____

Map 4:

1. Schema being explored:_____

2. Early Memory:_____

3. How I felt:_____

4. What I concluded:_____

5. Who was involved:_____

6. Environment:_____

7. Message learned:_____

Step 2: Identify Your Schema Reinforcers

- **Time Period:** *Elementary School*

- **Key Experience:** *Math class struggles*

- **People Involved:** *Teacher, classmates*

- **Actions that reinforced schema:**

    - *Teacher calling on others more*

    - *Being last to finish worksheets*

    - *Seeing others grasp concepts quickly What this confirmed: I'm not as smart How this affected me: Started avoiding participation*

Your Reinforcement Trackers:

Tracker 1:

- *Time Period:*_____
- *Key Experience:*_____
- *People Involved:*_____
- *Actions that reinforced schema:*_____

_____

_____

_____

- *What this confirmed:*_____
- *How this affected me:*_____

Tracker 2:

- *Time Period:*_____
- *Key Experience:*_____
- *People Involved:*_____
- *Actions that reinforced schema:*_____

_____

_____

_____

- *What this confirmed:*_____
- *How this affected me:*_____

Tracker 3:

- *Time Period:*_____

- *Key Experience:*_____

- *People Involved:*_____

- *Actions that reinforced schema:*_____

_____

_____

_____

- *What this confirmed:*_____

- *How this affected me:*_____

Step 3: Map Your Schema Environment

- **Location:** *Home*

- **Influential People:** *Parents*

- **Messages Received:**

  - *"Let me do it for you"*

  - *"Your sister does it better"*

  - *"Be careful, you might mess up"*

- **How often:** *Daily*

- **Impact level:** *Very strong Long-term effect: Learned to doubt abilities*

Your Environment Maps:

Map 1:

- *Location:*_____
- *Influential People:*_____
- *Messages Received:*_____

_____

_____

_____

- *How often:*_____
- *Impact level:*_____
- *Long-term effect:*_____

Map 2:

- *Location:*_____
- *Influential People:*_____
- *Messages Received:*_____

_____

_____

_____

- *How often:*_____
- *Impact level:*_____
- *Long-term effect:*_____

Step 4: Create Your Schema Maintenance Timeline

- **Age Range:** *12-14 years Schema-Supporting Behaviors:*
    - *Avoiding challenges*
    - *Comparing to others*
    - *Focusing on failures What kept it going:*
    - *Fear of mistakes*
    - *Seeking validation*
- **Self-critical thoughts Impact on choices:** *Stayed in comfort zone*

Your Maintenance Timelines:

- **Timeline 1:** *Age Range:_____Schema-Supporting Behaviors:*

  _____

  _____

    - *What kept it going:_____*

      _____

    - *Impact on choices:_____*

      _____

      _____

Your Maintenance Timelines:

- **Timeline 1:** *Age Range:*_____ *Schema-Supporting Behaviors:*

  _____

  _____

  - *What kept it going:*_____

    _____

  - *Impact on choices:*_____

    _____

    _____

Step 5: Identify Schema Challenges

- **Time Period:** High School Evidence Against Schema:
  - *Won art contest*
  - *Made honor roll*
- **Friends valued my advice Why I dismissed these:**
  - *"It was just luck"*
  - *"Others did better"*
  - *"They're just being nice" What this shows: Schema filtered out positives*

Your Challenge Identifications:

- **Challenge 1:** *Time Period:*_____*Evidence Against Schema:*

_____

_____

  - ◦ *Why I dismissed these:* _____

    _____

    _____

  - ◦ *What this shows:* _____

    _____

Your Challenge Identifications:

- **Challenge 2:** *Time Period:* _____ *Evidence Against Schema:*

_____

_____

  - ◦ *Why I dismissed these:* _____

    _____

    _____

  - ◦ *What this shows:* _____

    _____

Step 6: Create Your Schema Response Profile

- **Trigger Situation:** Group projects Automatic Thoughts:

  - *"I'll slow everyone down"*

  - *"They won't want my ideas"*

  - *"I'll make mistakes"*

- **Physical Response:** *Tense shoulders, racing heart*

- **Emotional Response:** *Anxiety, shame*

- **Behavioral Response:** *Took smallest role possible*

- **Alternative View:** *Everyone has different strengths*

Your Response Profiles:

- **Profile 1:** *Trigger Situation:*_____ *Automatic Thoughts:*

  _____

  _____

- **Physical Response:**_____

- **Emotional Response:**_____

- **Behavioral Response:**_____

- **Alternative View:**_____

Your Response Profiles:

- **Profile 2:** *Trigger Situation:*_____ *Automatic Thoughts:*

_____

_____

- **Physical Response:**_____

- **Emotional Response:**_____

- **Behavioral Response:**_____

- **Alternative View:**_____

Your Response Profiles:

- **Profile 3:** *Trigger Situation:*_____ *Automatic Thoughts:*

_____

_____

- **Physical Response:**_____

- **Emotional Response:**_____

- **Behavioral Response:**_____

- **Alternative View:**_____

<u>Pro Tips:</u>
- *Be specific with examples*
- *Notice patterns across time periods*
- *Include both major and minor incidents*
- *Consider different environments*
- *Look for repeated messages*
- *Track how the schema adapted over time*

<u>**Remember:**</u> *Understanding your schema's origins helps you see it as learned, not fact!*

Schema Behavior Pattern

Purpose:

To identify and track your schema-driven behaviors and develop healthier responses.

Materials Needed:

- Pen or pencil
- Willingness to observe your behaviors

Real-Life Application

Alex noticed his *"Unrelenting Standards"* schema made him overwork himself. When assigned a group project, he'd stay up late redoing others' work. By tracking this pattern, he learned to balance high standards with trust in his teammates.

Step 1: Identify Your Schema's Warning Signs

Your body and emotions often try to tell you when a schema is being triggered. Think of these as your personal "early warning system." Just like your phone sends notifications, your body and emotions send you signals that something's up!

First, let's check what your body tells you. Think about a time when you were upset or stressed. What did you notice in your body? **Check all that apply:**

Physical Signs:

- *Tense shoulders (feeling like you're carrying a heavy backpack)*
- *Racing heart (feels like you just ran up stairs)*
- *Stomach knots (butterflies or upset feeling)*
- *Shallow breathing (hard to take deep breaths)*
- *Headaches (pressure or pain in your head)*
- *Other:* _____

Now, what emotions pop up? These are your emotional notifications:

- *Anxiety (worried, nervous)*
- *Anger (frustrated, mad)*
- *Sadness (down, gloomy)*
- *Fear (scared, afraid)*
- *Shame (feeling bad about yourself)*
- *Other:* _____

> **Pro Tip:** *The more signs you can identify, the better you'll get at catching your schema early - like spotting storm clouds before it rains!*

Step 2: Behavior Pattern Analysis

Think of this like being a detective investigating your own pattern. We're going to map out how your schema works, just like tracking the path of a pinball in a pinball machine!

First, write down which schema you're investigating:

My Schema: _____

(Not sure? Look back at the schema types we discussed earlier in the chapter!)

Trigger Situation

Automatic Thoughts

Emotional Response

Behavioral Response

Now, let's break down your pattern. Use these prompts to help you fill in each section:

Trigger Situations:

- (What situations set off your schema? **Example:** *"When someone doesn't text back"* or *"When I have to present in class"*)

_____

_____

_____

Automatic Thoughts:

- (What thoughts pop into your head instantly? **Example:** *"They must hate me"* or *"I'm going to mess up"*)

_____

_____

_____

Emotional Response:

- (How do these thoughts make you feel? **Example:** *"Scared and nervous"* or *"Angry and hurt"*)

_____

_____

_____

Behavioral Response:

- (What do you usually do next? **Example:** *"Send multiple texts"* or *"Pretend to be sick to avoid class"*)

_____

_____

_____

Remember: *There's no "wrong" answer here - you're just observing your pattern like a scientist studying something interesting!*

Step 3: Develop Healthier Responses

Now that you know your pattern, let's create a new game plan! Think of this like creating a new playlist to replace one you've outgrown.

When I notice my schema activated, **I will:**

- Instead of (current behavior):

(Write down what you usually do - be honest, this is your old playlist!)

Example: *"Sending angry texts"* or *"Giving up on the assignment"*

_____

_____

_____

- I will try (new behavior):

(What's a better way to handle it? Think of what a confident, calm version of you would do)

Example: *"Take three deep breaths and wait 10 minutes before texting"* or *"Break the assignment into smaller parts"*

_____

_____

_____

- Support I need to make this change:

(What tools, people, or reminders would help you stick to your new plan?)

Example: *"Set a timer on my phone"* or *"Ask my friend to check in on me"*

_____

_____

_____

Pro Tip: *Start small! Pick one situation to practice your new response. It's like learning a new TikTok dance - you've got to practice the moves before you can nail the whole routine!*

Schema Support Network

Purpose:

To build a support system that helps you challenge and modify your schemas.

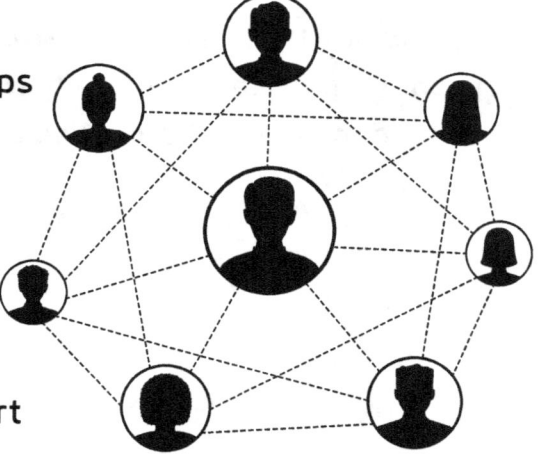

Materials Needed:

- Pen or pencil
- Contact information for support people

Real-Life Application

Maya struggled with her *"Defectiveness"* schema but built a strong support network. When negative thoughts arose, she had specific people to reach out to - her counselor for professional guidance, her best friend for encouragement, and her art teacher who always helped her see her creative strengths.

Step 1: Map Your Support Network

Inner Circle
(Closest
Support)

Regular
Support

ME

Occasional
Support

Professional
Support

Emergency
Support

Step 2: Support Contact List

Name	Relationship	Type of Support They Provide	Best Way to Contact	Best Times to Reach Out
Sarah Johnson	School Counselor	Professional guidance and coping strategies	Email or office hours	Weekdays 8am-3pm

Step 3: Create Your Support Plan

When I notice my schema is triggered, I will:

First step:

_____

_____

<u>Example:</u> *"Take a deep breath and remind myself that my thoughts are not always facts."*

If that doesn't help, I will:

_____

_____

<u>Example:</u> *"Write down what I'm feeling or text a trusted friend for perspective."*

If I need more support, I will:

_____

_____

<u>Example:</u> *"Talk to a mentor, counselor, or someone I trust about what's going on."*

Emergency Plan:

_____

_____

<u>Example:</u> *"Step away from the situation, count to ten, or do a grounding exercise like naming five things I see."*

Step 4: Support Agreement

I commit to:

- *Reaching out when I need help*
- *Being honest about my struggles*
- *Following through with suggestions*
- *Showing appreciation for support*
- *Taking responsibility for my growth*

Signature:_____ **Date:** _____/_____/_____

Support Person Signature:_____ **Date:** _____/_____/_____

Chapter 1 Reflection

Take a moment to reflect on what you've learned about your schemas:

The most important thing I learned was:

_____

_____

_____

I plan to work on this schema first:

_____

_____

_____

My biggest challenge will be:

_____

_____

_____

I feel prepared to handle this because:

_____

_____

_____

Chapter 2

Metacognitive Skills

"The mind is not a vessel to be filled but a fire to be kindled."
- Plutarch

Understanding Metacognition

Think of metacognition as being the director of your own mind's movie. It's not just about having thoughts - it's about understanding how and why you think the way you do. Pretty cool, right?

Real-Life Application:

Imagine you're studying for a test. Instead of just reading your notes over and over, you stop and think, *"Wait, is this method actually helping me learn?"* That's metacognition in action! You're thinking about your thinking, like having a mental coach in your head.

Why Metacognition Matters

When you develop strong metacognitive skills, you can:

- *Figure out the best way YOUR brain learns*
- *Catch unhelpful thoughts before they spiral*
- *Choose better strategies for solving problems*
- *Understand why you feel the way you feel*
- *Make better decisions*

The Three Parts of Metacognition

1. **Planning (Before):** *Like checking the weather before deciding what to wear*
2. **Monitoring (During):** *Like keeping an eye on your phone's battery level*
3. **Evaluating (After):** *Like watching a replay to improve your gaming strategy*

Let's explore these skills through six engaging exercises that will help you become the boss of your own brain!

Thought Observer Training

Purpose:

To develop your "mental camera" - learning to observe your thoughts without getting caught up in them.

Materials Needed:

- Pen or pencil
- Timer (phone works great!)
- Quiet space where you won't be interrupted

Think of this like becoming a wildlife photographer, but instead of watching animals, you're watching your thoughts in their natural habitat!

Step 1: Thought Spotting Practice (5 minutes)

First, let's do a quick practice round. Set your timer for 1 minute and just watch what thoughts pop into your head. Don't try to change them - just notice them, like watching clouds float by.

Now, check which types of thoughts you spotted:

To-do list items ("I need to...")

☐ *Worries about the future*

☐ *Memories from the past*

☐ *Random observations*

☐ *Feelings about yourself*

☐ *Plans or goals*

☐ *Other:*_____

Step 2: Detailed Thought Photography

Pick one thought that keeps showing up in your mind lately. Let's capture it in detail:

The thought is:
(Write it exactly as it appears in your mind - like taking a clear photo)

_____

_____

When does this thought usually show up?
(What's happening when you notice it?)

_____

_____

How strong is this thought?
Draw an X on the line:

Very Quiet ---|------------------|--- Very Loud

What color would this thought be?_____
(This helps you recognize it more easily next time!)

What do you usually do when this thought appears?

_____

_____

Step 3: Develop Your Observer Skills

Now that you've practiced spotting thoughts, let's create your personal thought

Observer Toolkit:

Thought Type	How it Shows Up	Observer Strategy
Example: *Worry thoughts*	**Example:** Racing heart, mind spinning	**Example:** Name it: "Oh, there's my worry brain again"

Pro Tip: *The more you practice observing your thoughts without getting tangled in them, the easier it becomes. It's like learning to watch a scary movie - at first, you might get super caught up in it, but eventually, you can remind yourself "This is just a movie" (or in this case, "These are just thoughts").*

Thought Detective Agency

Purpose:

To investigate your thoughts like a detective solving a case, finding clues about where they come from and if they're telling the truth.

Materials Needed:

- Pen or pencil
- Your detective mindset
- Willingness to look for evidence

Real-Life Application

Jamie kept thinking "Nobody wants to be my friend." But when they investigated like a detective, they found evidence that wasn't true: they had two text invites that week and a lunch buddy at school. Being a thought detective helped them see the whole picture!

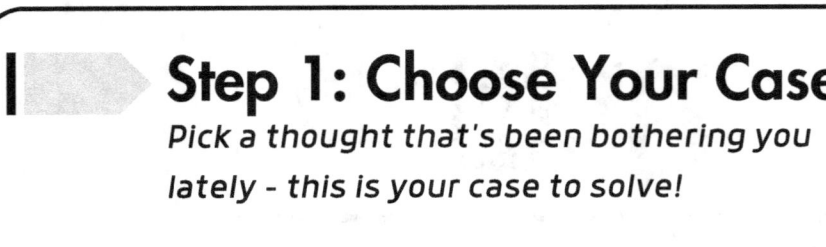

Step 1: Choose Your Case

Pick a thought that's been bothering you lately - this is your case to solve!

Write your "suspect thought" here:
(The thought you want to investigate)

_____

_____

Rate how much you believe this thought right now:

Not at all true ☐ 1 ☐ 2 ☐ 3 ☐ 4 ☐ 5 **Totally true**

Step 2: Gather Evidence

Like any good detective, we need to look at ALL the evidence, not just what seems obvious at first!

Evidence that supports the thought:
(What makes you think it might be true?)

Cue 1:_____

Cue 2:_____

Cue 3:_____

Evidence that doesn't support the thought:
[What suggests it might not be completely true?]

Cue 1:_____

Cue 2:_____

Cue 3:_____

Step 3: Interview Your Witnesses

Who else could give you perspective on this thought? Think about:

☐ *A good friend*

☐ *A family member who supports you*

☐ *A teacher or counselor*

☐ *Your past self*

☐ *Your future self*

What would they say about your thought?

_____

_____

Step 4: Solve the Case

Now that you've gathered all the evidence, let's solve this case!

What's a more balanced way to look at this situation?
(Like a detective writing their final report)

_____

_____

_____

Rate how much you believe the original thought now:

Not at all true ☐ 1 ☐ 2 ☐ 3 ☐ 4 ☐ 5 **Totally true**

<u>Pro Tip:</u> *Keep this detective skill handy! Next time a troubling thought pops up, remember to gather evidence before jumping to conclusions.*

Metacognitive Weather Report

Purpose:

To track your thought patterns like a meteorologist tracks weather patterns, helping you predict and prepare for different "thought weather."

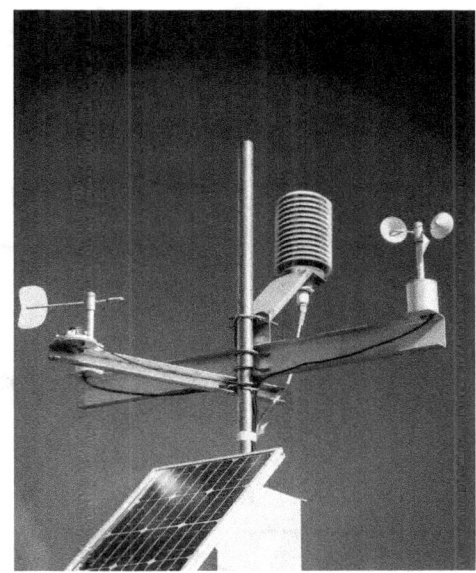

Materials Needed:

- Pen or pencil
- Your observation skills
- Openness to noticing patterns

Real-Life Application

Sofia noticed her thoughts were like weather patterns - sometimes sunny and clear, sometimes stormy with worried thoughts. By tracking these patterns, she learned that her thoughts usually got "stormy" before big tests, so she could prepare better coping strategies in advance.

Step 1: Create Your Thought Weather Scale

Pick a thought that's been bothering you lately - this is your case to solve!

 Sunny *(Clear, positive thoughts)*

 Partly Cloudy *(Mild worries)*

 Cloudy *(Confused, mixed thoughts)*

 **Stormy** *(Strong negative thoughts)*

 Foggy *(Unclear, scattered thoughts)*

Step 2: Daily Weather Tracking

Days of the week across the top

Time Periods:	Mon	Tue	Weds	Thurs	Fri	Sat	Sun
Morning ☀	☐	☐	☐	☐	☐	☐	☐
Afternoon ☀	☐	☐	☐	☐	☐	☐	☐
Evening 🌙	☐	☐	☐	☐	☐	☐	☐

Step 3: Notice Your Weather Patterns

What makes your thoughts:

Sunny? *(When do you have your clearest, most positive thoughts?)*

_____

_____

Stormy? *(What tends to bring on negative thought storms?)*

_____

_____

Foggy? *(When do you feel most confused or scattered?)*

_____

_____

Step 4: Create Your Weather Preparation Kit

Just like you might pack an umbrella when rain is forecast, what can you prepare for each type of thought weather?

For Stormy Thoughts:
(Example: "Listen to my calm playlist, text my best friend")

_____

_____

For Foggy Thoughts:
(Example: "Take a walk, make a simple to-do list")

_____

_____

For Cloudy Thoughts:
(Example: "Do some deep breathing, talk to Mom")

_____

_____

Pro Tip: *Remember, just like real weather, thought weather changes! No stormy period lasts forever, and you can learn to handle any kind of mental weather that comes your way.*

Thought Sorting Station

Purpose:

To organize your thoughts like sorting items in your closet, making it easier to see what's helpful and what's not.

Materials Needed:

- Pen or pencil
- Your sorting skills
- Willingness to organize your thoughts

Real-Life Application

Dylan's mind was cluttered with thoughts about an upcoming dance. By sorting them into different categories (like "Helpful Planning Thoughts" vs. "Unhelpful Worry Thoughts"), they could focus on the useful ones and let go of the rest - just like keeping favorite clothes and donating ones that don't fit anymore.

Step 1: Collect Your Thoughts

Take 5 minutes to write down all the thoughts going through your mind right now. Don't judge them - just write them down like making a quick list:

_____

_____

_____

_____

_____

Step 2: Create Your Sorting Bins

- **Helpful Now** *(Thoughts that help you in the present)*

_____

_____

_____

- **Save for Later** *(Thoughts to think about another time)*

_____

_____

_____

- **Not Useful** *(Thoughts that don't help at all)*

_____

_____

_____

- **Need More Info** *(Thoughts you're not sure about yet)*

_____

_____

_____

Now sort your thoughts from Step 1 into these bins. Like sorting through apps on your phone - some you use daily, some you might need later, some you can delete!

Step 3: Thought Quality Check

For each thought in your "Helpful Now" bin, rate it:

- *Is this thought based on facts?* ☐ Yes ☐ No
- *Does it help me take positive action?* ☐ Yes ☐ No
- *Would I say this to a friend?* ☐ Yes ☐ No
- *Does it match my values?* ☐ Yes ☐ No
- *Is it kind to myself?* ☐ Yes ☐ No

Step 4: Create Your "Keep vs. Delete" List

Just like decluttering your phone's photo gallery, let's decide what to keep and what to let go:

- **Thoughts to Keep:** *(These help you or make you stronger)*

1. _____

2. _____

3. _____

- **Thoughts to Delete:** *(These hold you back or bring you down)*

1. _____

2. _____

3. _____

Pro Tip: *You don't have to keep every thought that pops into your head - just like you don't keep every notification on your phone!*

Mind Laboratory Experiments

Purpose:

To test your thoughts like a scientist tests hypotheses, helping you discover what's really true.

Materials Needed:

- Pen or pencil
- Your scientist mindset
- Curiosity to experiment

Real-Life Application

Maria thought "I'm bad at making friends" but decided to test this thought with an experiment. She hypothesized that if she smiled at five people each day for a week, no one would smile back. The results surprised her - 80% of people smiled back, proving her thought wasn't accurate!

Step 1: Choose Your Experiment

Pick a thought you want to test:

_____

_____

Your hypothesis *(what you think will happen):*

_____

_____

How sure are you about your hypothesis?

Not at all sure ☐ 1 ☐ 2 ☐ 3 ☐ 4 ☐ 5 Very sure

Step 2: Design Your Experiment

What could you do to test if this thought is true?
(Think small, safe experiments you can try in daily life)

- **Experiment idea:**

_____

_____

- **How will you measure the results?**

_____

_____

Days of the week	What you tried	What happened	How you felt

Step 3: Safety Guidelines

Before you start, check:

- ☐ *Is this experiment safe to try?*
- ☐ *Could I handle a "no" result?*
- ☐ *Do I need any support to try this?*
- ☐ *What's my backup plan if needed?*

Step 4: Run Your Experiment

Time period:_____
(Start with a short time, like one week)

Data Collection:
(What actually happened? Be specific like a scientist!)

_____

_____

_____

Step 5: Analyze Your Results

What did you learn?

_____

_____

Was your hypothesis correct?

☐ Yes ☐ No ☐ Partly

How does this change your original thought?

_____

_____

Pro Tip: *Real scientists don't expect to be right all the time - they learn from every experiment, whether it proves or disproves their hypothesis. Your thought experiments are the same way!*

Metacognitive Tool Belt

Purpose:

To build your personal collection of thinking tools, like having the right app for every situation on your phone.

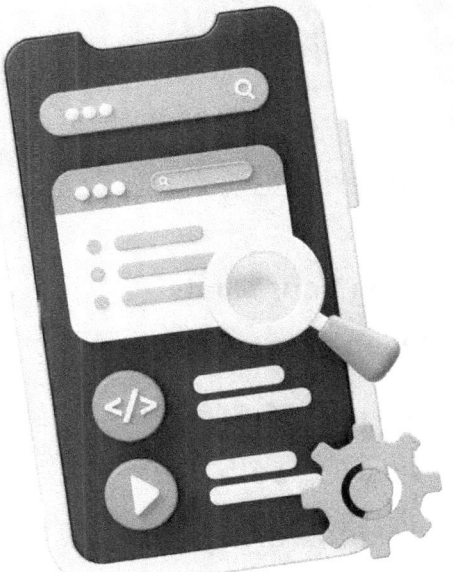

Materials Needed:

- Pen or pencil
- Your experience from previous exercises
- Creativity to customize your tools

Real-Life Application

Chris felt overwhelmed by different situations until they created their "thinking tool belt." Before a presentation, they used their "Thought Detective" tool to challenge nervous thoughts. During friend drama, they pulled out their "Weather Report" tool to track their emotional storms. Having the right tool for each situation made them feel more confident!

Step 1: Stock Your Tool Belt

Let's gather all the thinking tools you've learned. Check the ones you find most helpful:

For Analyzing Thoughts:

- ☐ *Thought Detective (finding evidence)*
- ☐ *Weather Tracking (monitoring patterns)*
- ☐ *Thought Sorting (organizing mental clutter)*
- ☐ *Mind Experiments (testing beliefs)*
- ☐ *Other:_____*

For Calming Your Mind:

- ☐ *Deep breathing*
- ☐ *Grounding exercises*
- ☐ *Positive self-talk*
- ☐ *Taking a break*
- ☐ *Other:_____*

For Problem Solving:

- ☐ *Breaking things down*
- ☐ *Getting another perspective*
- ☐ *Making a pro/con list*
- ☐ *Testing solutions*
- ☐ *Other:_____*

Step 2: Create Your Quick-Access Tools

Fill in your favorite quick tools:

- **THINK:** *(Tools for managing thoughts)*

1 _____

2. _____

3. _____

- **FEEL:** *(Tools for handling emotions)*

1 _____

2. _____

3. _____

- **DO:** *(Actions that help)*

1 _____

2. _____

3. _____

Metacognitive Skills

Step 3: Match Tools to Situations

Let's practice choosing the right tool for different scenarios.
What would you use if...

You're worried about a test tomorrow:

Tool choice:_____

Why this tool?_____

You're feeling left out of a friend group:

Tool choice:_____

Why this tool?_____

You're feeling left out of a friend group:

Tool choice:_____

Why this tool?_____

Metacognitive Skills

Step 4: Create Your Emergency Kit

Sometimes you need your tools quickly! Let's make a mini emergency kit:

- **My go-to emergency tools are:**

1 _____

2. _____

3. _____

Where I'll keep my emergency kit:

_____

Pro Tip: *Just like you probably have favorite apps you use most on your phone, you'll probably find yourself using certain thinking tools more than others - that's totally normal! The important thing is having options when you need them.*

Metacognitive Skills

Chapter 2 Reflection

Take a moment to think about your metacognitive journey:

The most useful thing I learned was:

_____

_____

_____

The tool I'll probably use most is:

_____

_____

_____

I was surprised to discover:

_____

_____

_____

In the future, I want to work on:

_____

_____

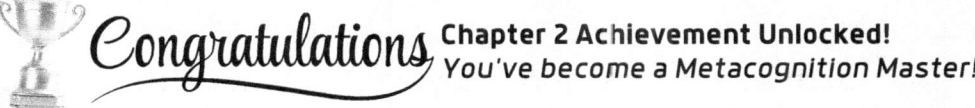

Congratulations **Chapter 2 Achievement Unlocked!**
You've become a Metacognition Master!

Pro Tip for Using Chapter 2: *Remember, becoming aware of your thoughts is like learning any new skill - it takes practice! Don't worry if it feels weird at first. The more you use these tools, the more natural they'll feel.*

Chapter 3

Advanced Emotional Regulation

"The greatest discovery of my generation is that human beings can alter their lives by altering their attitudes of mind."

- Williams James

Understanding Advanced Emotional Regulation

Think of your emotions like a powerful gaming system - they can run all kinds of programs (from excitement to anger to joy), but you need the right controls to play the game well. Advanced emotional regulation is like leveling up from being a casual gamer to becoming a pro player!

Real-Life Application:

Kai used to get overwhelmed by intense emotions, like when their team lost an important game. After learning advanced regulation skills, they could recognize their disappointment, let themselves feel it for a bit, then consciously shift into "next steps" mode - like planning extra practice sessions. It wasn't about not feeling disappointed; it was about managing that feeling productively.

Why Advanced Regulation Matters

Basic emotion regulation is like having a simple volume control - turn emotions up or down. Advanced regulation gives you a whole mixing board of controls:

- Intensity *(how strong the emotion feels)*
- Duration *(how long it lasts)*
- Expression *(how you show it)*
- Transition *(how you move between emotions)*
- Integration *(how you handle mixed emotions)*

Emotion Mapping System

Purpose:

To create a detailed map of your emotional landscape, like having a high-resolution GPS for your feelings.

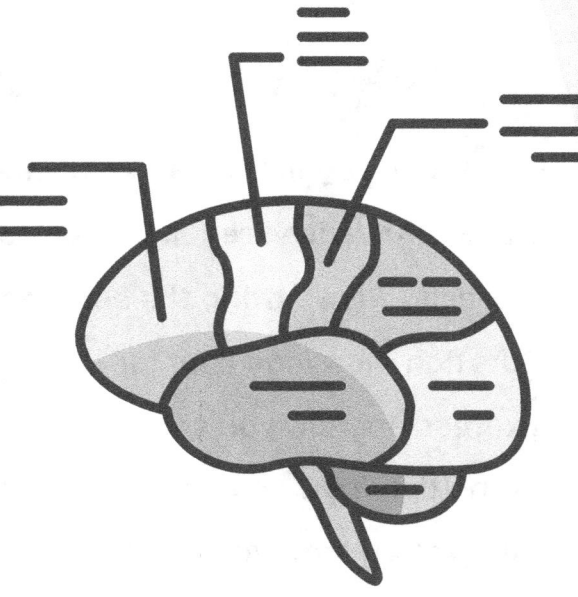

Materials Needed:

- Pen or pencil
- Your emotional awareness
- Willingness to explore feelings deeply

Real-Life Application

Mia thought she just got "mad" at her siblings. When she mapped her emotions, she discovered her anger usually started as frustration when she felt ignored, then built up if she didn't address it early. This map helped her catch the frustration early and speak up before it turned into anger!

Step 1: Create Your Base Map

Let's start by identifying your emotional range. Think of this like mapping out different territories in your emotional world.

Primary Emotions I Experience Most:
(Check all that apply and add intensity rating 1-5)

Happiness Family:
- ☐ Joy
- ☐ Excitement
- ☐ Contentment
- ☐ Pride
- ☐ Other:_____

Anger Family:
- ☐ Frustration
- ☐ Irritation
- ☐ Rage
- ☐ Resentment
- ☐ Other:_____

Fear Family:
- ☐ Anxiety
- ☐ Worry
- ☐ Panic
- ☐ Nervousness
- ☐ Other:_____

Sadness Family:

- ☐ *Disappointment*
- ☐ *Grief*
- ☐ *Loneliness*
- ☐ *Hopelessness*
- ☐ *Other:*_____

Step 2: Map Your Emotion Patterns

_____   Happiness | Anger   _____

_____   Fear | Sadness   _____

_____

Now, plot your common emotional experiences on the map:

1. Start with a recent emotion: _____

2. Mark where it started on the map

3. Draw its path (how it moved between emotions)

4. Note what triggered each shift

Step 3: Identify Your Emotional Highways

What patterns do you notice? Like a traffic map,
which emotional routes do you travel most often?

My most common emotional paths are:

(Example: "Nervousness   Frustration   Anger")

1. _____

2. _____

3. _____

What usually triggers these paths?

_____

_____

What helps you take better routes?

_____

_____

Step 4: Create Navigation Shortcuts

For each common emotional path, let's create a better route:

Starting Emotion	Usually Leads To	Better Route to Take	Tools/Support Needed

Pro Tip: *Just like a GPS offers alternate routes when there's traffic, you can create alternate paths for your emotions when you notice you're heading down a challenging road!*

Emotion-Body Connection Lab

Purpose:

To understand how your emotions show up in your body, like creating a detailed user manual for your emotional-physical responses.

Materials Needed:

- Pen or pencil
- Body awareness
- Curiosity about your physical responses

Real-Life Application

Jordan never understood why they got headaches before big social events until they mapped their anxiety in their body. They discovered their shoulders tensed up first, then their jaw clenched, and finally came the headache. By noticing the shoulder tension early, they could prevent the headache by stretching and relaxing!

Step 1: Create Your Body-Emotion Map

Using different colors or symbols, mark where you feel different emotions in your body:

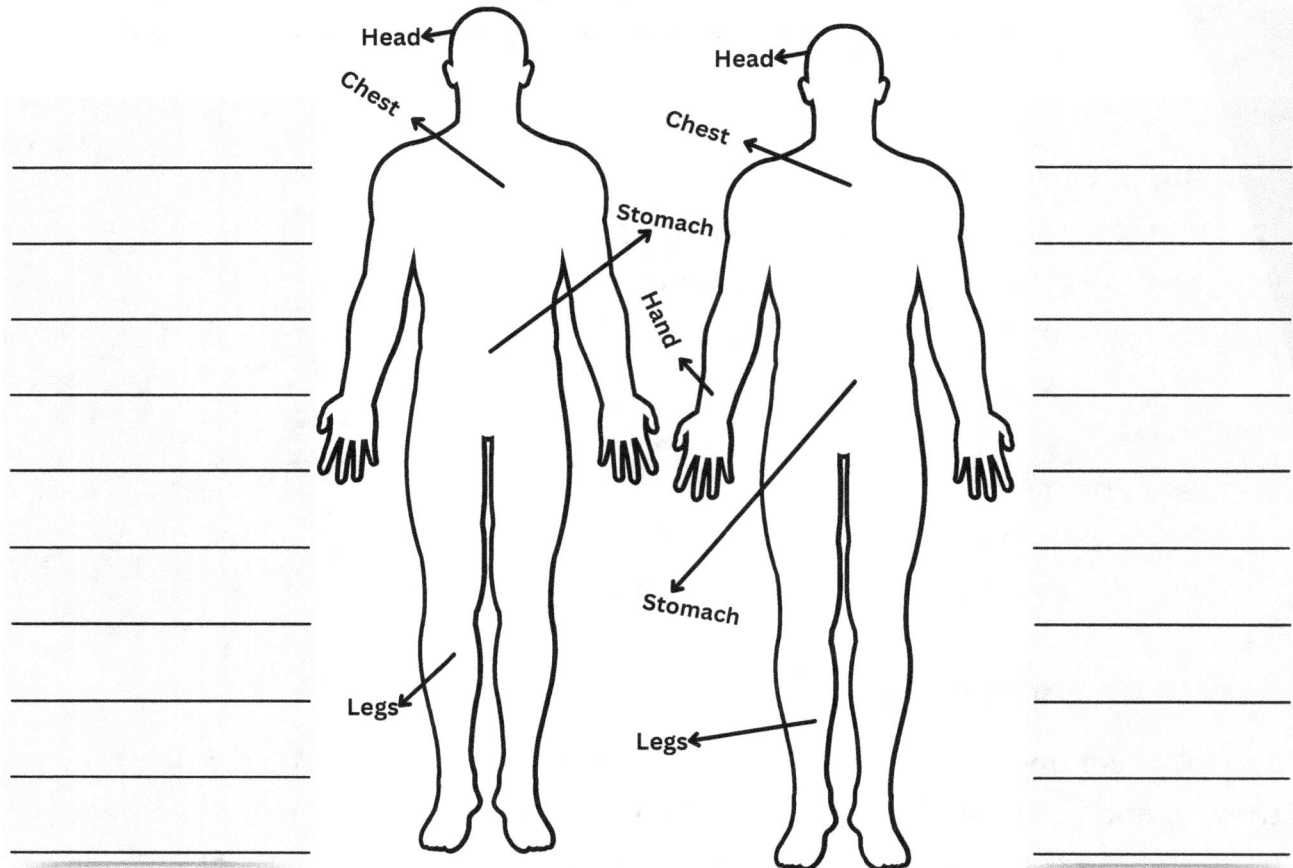

_____

_____

_____

_____

_____

_____

_____

_____

_____

Pleasant Emotions:

- *Happiness (Example: warm chest, relaxed shoulders)*
- *Excitement (Example: fluttery stomach, energized legs)*
- *Pride (Example: tall posture, lifted chin)*
- *Peace (Example: relaxed muscles, calm breathing)*

Unpleasant Emotions:

- *Anxiety (Example: tight chest, racing heart)*
- *Anger (Example: hot face, clenched fists)*
- *Sadness (Example: heavy limbs, tired eyes)*
- *Fear (Example: tense shoulders, shallow breathing)*

Step 2: Track Your Physical Warning Signs

Your body often knows you're having an emotion before your mind catches up. Let's identify your early warning signs:

Head Region:
- ☐ Headache
- ☐ Clenched jaw
- ☐ Furrowed brow
- ☐ Other: _____

Chest Region:
- ☐ Racing heart
- ☐ Tight chest
- ☐ Changed breathing
- ☐ Other: _____

Stomach Region:
- ☐ Butterflies
- ☐ Nausea
- ☐ Hunger changes
- ☐ Other: _____

Muscles:
- ☐ Tension
- ☐ Weakness
- ☐ Trembling
- ☐ Other: _____

Step 3: Create Your Body Reset Buttons

Just like a game controller has buttons for different actions, your body has specific "reset buttons" for different emotional states. Let's find yours:

- **When I feel anxious, these physical actions help:**

1. _____

2. _____

3. _____

- **When I feel angry, these physical actions help:**

1. _____

2. _____

3. _____

- **When I feel sad, these physical actions help:**

1. _____

2. _____

3. _____

Step 4: Design Your Physical Intervention Plan

Fill in your intervention cards:

Card 1:

When I notice: _____

I will: _____

Card 2:

When I notice: _____

I will: _____

Card 3:

When I notice: _____

I will: _____

Card 4:

When I notice: _____

I will: _____

Card 5:

When I notice: _____

I will: _____

Card 6:

When I notice: _____

I will: _____

Advanced Emotional Regulation

Step 5: Practice Your Body Awareness

Set 3 times during the day to do a quick body scan:

- **Morning time:**_____
- **Afternoon time:**_____
- **Evening time:**_____

During each scan, notice:
- ☐ *Areas of tension*
- ☐ *Energy level*
- ☐ *Emotional state*
- ☐ *Physical needs*

	Mon	Tues	Weds	Thurs	Fri	Sat	Sun
Morning:							
Afternoon:							
Evening:							

<u>**Example:**</u> **Monday Morning:** *Tight shoulders, anxious about test*

<u>**Pro Tip**</u>*: Your body is always giving you information about your emotions - like having a built-in mood ring! The better you get at reading these signals, the earlier you can take action to regulate your emotions.*

Emotion Regulation Toolbox

Purpose:

To build a personalized collection of emotion regulation strategies, like creating your own emotional first-aid kit.

Materials Needed:

- Pen or pencil
- Your experiences with different strategies
- Creative thinking cap

Real-Life Application

Liam used to only have one way to deal with strong emotions - listening to music. While this helped sometimes, it wasn't enough for every situation. After building his emotion regulation toolbox, he had different strategies for different emotional needs - like using breathing exercises for anxiety, journaling for sadness, and exercise for anger. Having multiple tools made him feel more confident in handling any emotion!

Step 1: Assess Your Current Tools

Let's start by looking at what's already in your emotional toolbox:

When I feel strong emotions, I usually:

- *Listen to music*
- *Talk to friends*
- *Exercise*
- *Cry*
- *Get angry*
- *Withdraw*
- *Other:* _____

Rate how well these work:

Great tool ☐ 3 ☐ 2 ☐ 1 ☐ 0 **Not helpful**

Step 2: Expand Your Toolbox

Let's organize tools by what they do best:

Quick Calm-Down Tools:
(Tools that work in 5 minutes or less)

1. _____

2. _____

3. _____

Deep Processing Tools:
(Tools for when you have more time to work through emotions)

1. _____

2. _____

3. _____

Prevention Tools:
(Tools to use daily to stay emotionally balanced)

1. _____

2. _____

3. _____

Step 3: Create Specialized Tool Kits

Fill in each kit with tools that work for that specific situation:

School Stress Kit

Friend Drama Kit

Quick Tool:_____

Processing Tool:_____

Prevention Tool:_____

Quick Tool:_____

Processing Tool:_____

Prevention Tool:_____

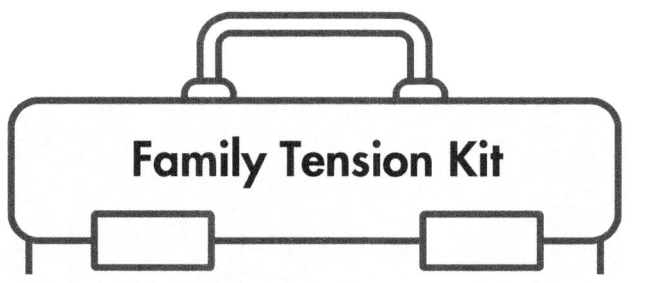

Family Tension Kit

Quick Tool:_____

Processing Tool:_____

Prevention Tool:_____

Personal Pressure Kit

Quick Tool:_____

Processing Tool:_____

Prevention Tool:_____

Step 4: Tool Testing Lab

Before using a tool in a real situation, let's test it out:

Pick a new tool to try:_____

When will you test it?_____

Success looks like:_____

After testing:

- *What worked?*_____

- *What didn't?*_____

- *Changes needed?*_____

Advanced Emotional Regulation

Step 5: Create Your Emergency Protocol

Sometimes emotions are overwhelming and you need a clear plan.
Let's create your step-by-step emergency response:

 **Warning Signs**

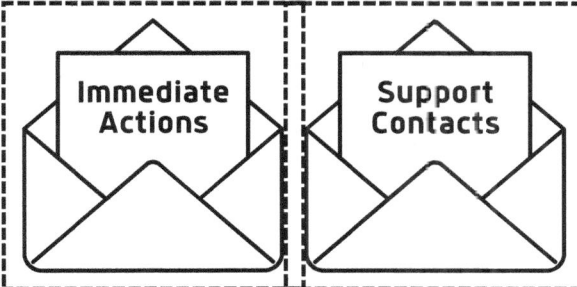 **Immediate Actions**   **Support Contacts**

 **Reminder Statements**

Fill in your emergency protocol:

- **I know I need emergency help when:** _____

  _____

- **Step 1: Immediate action** _____

  _____

- **Step 2: If that doesn't work** _____

  _____

- **Step 3: People to contact** _____

  _____

- **Reminder to self:** _____

  _____

Pro Tip: *Think of your emotion regulation tools like apps on your phone - some you'll use every day, others you'll need for specific situations, and some are just for emergencies. The key is knowing which tool to use when!*

Advanced Emotional Regulation

Advanced Emotion Navigation

Purpose:

To develop skilled navigation of complex emotional situations, like having an advanced GPS for your feelings.

Materials Needed:

- Pen or pencil
- Your emotional awareness
- Willingness to explore deeper emotional patterns

Real-Life Application

Tasha used to get stuck in a loop when feeling jealous of her friend's social media posts. After learning advanced emotion navigation, she could recognize that her jealousy was actually a mix of admiration and insecurity. This understanding helped her channel those feelings into inspiration for her own goals instead of getting caught in negative thoughts.

Step 1: Map Your Emotional Combinations

Sometimes emotions come in layers, like a smoothie with different ingredients. Let's identify your common blends:

Check the emotion combinations you experience:

- ☐ *Angry + Hurt*
- ☐ *Excited + Nervous*
- ☐ *Happy + Guilty*
- ☐ *Proud + Worried*
- ☐ *Other:*

Pick your most challenging combination:

- *Primary emotion:* _____
- *Secondary emotion:* _____
- *How they mix together:* _____

Step 2: Create Your Navigation Routes

For your chosen emotion combination:

Destination (Desired Emotional State)

Checkpoints (Navigation Steps) -

- Starting point (Initial Emotion)

Starting Point:

- *I first feel:*_____

- *Because:*_____

Checkpoint 1: Awareness

- *I notice this physically by:*_____

- *I notice this mentally by:*_____

Checkpoint 2: Understanding

- *This combination usually means:*_____

- *It's trying to tell me:*_____

Checkpoint 3: Choice Point

- *I could react by:*_____

- *Or I could respond by:*_____

Destination:

- *I want to feel:*_____

- *I can get there by:*_____

Step 3: Advanced Navigation Skills Practice

Let's practice handling tricky emotional situations:

<u>**Here is an example:**</u>

- **Scenario 1:** *Mixed Messages When someone says they're "fine" but seem mad:*
    - **My emotional response:** *I feel confused and worried because their body language doesn't match their words.*
    - **Navigation strategy:** *"I notice something seems off. I'm here if you want to talk, or we can just hang out quietly."*

Scenario 1: *Mixed Messages*

- **When someone says they're "fine" but seem mad:**

    - My emotional response:_____

    - Navigation strategy:_____

Scenario 2: *Emotional Conflict*

- **When you feel happy about something but others are sad:**

    - My emotional response:_____

    - Navigation strategy:_____

Scenario 3: *Delayed Emotions*

- **When you feel okay during a challenge but crash afterward:**

    - My emotional response:_____

    - Navigation strategy:_____

Step 4: Create Your Navigation Tools

Choose a primary emotion and what it often combines with then choose your best navigation tool, and a reminder of what to do.

Fill in your navigation cards:

- **Card 1:** *Primary Emotion*
- **Name:**_____
- **Often combines with:**_____
- **Best navigation tools:**_____
- **Remember to:**_____

- **Card 2:** *Primary Emotion*
- **Name:**_____
- **Often combines with:**_____
- **Best navigation tools:**_____
- **Remember to:**_____

- **Card 3:** *Primary Emotion*
- **Name:**_____
- **Often combines with:**_____
- **Best navigation tools:**_____
- **Remember to:**_____

Advanced Emotional Regulation

Step 5: Practice Complex Navigation

Choose a recent situation where you felt multiple emotions:

What happened:

_____

_____

Emotions involved:

1._____

2._____

3._____

How they interacted:

_____

_____

What you'll try next time:

_____

_____

Pro Tip: *Think of emotional navigation like playing a complex video game - at first, the controls seem complicated, but with practice, they become natural. Don't worry if you don't handle every situation perfectly; each experience helps you level up your skills!*

Emotion-Thought Connection

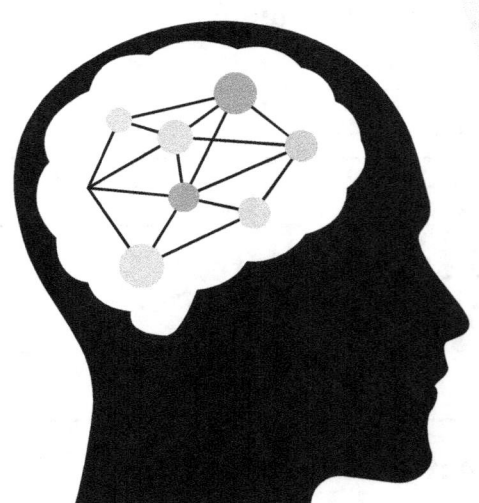

Purpose:

To understand how your thoughts and emotions work together, like understanding the code behind a computer program.

Materials Needed:

- Pen or pencil
- Your observation skills
- Curiosity about your thought patterns

Real-Life Application

Devon noticed they always felt terrible after scrolling social media. By exploring the emotion-thought connection, they discovered specific thoughts ("Everyone else is having more fun" and "I'm missing out") were triggering feelings of loneliness and anxiety. Understanding this connection helped them either challenge these thoughts or limit social media when feeling vulnerable.

Step 1: Identify Your Thought-Emotion Loops

Let's track some common loops:

Loop 1: Social Situations

- **Thought:**_____
- **Leads to feeling:**_____
- **Which makes me:**_____
- **Replace with a New Positive Thought:**_____

Loop 2: Performance (School/Sports/Activities)

- **Thought:**_____
- **Leads to feeling:**_____
- **Which makes me:**_____
- **Replace with a New Positive Thought:**_____

Loop 3: Relationships

- **Thought:**_____
- **Leads to feeling:**_____
- **Which makes me:**_____
- **Replace with a New Positive Thought:**_____

Step 2: Find Your Power Points

In each loop you identified, mark where you have the most power to make changes:

- ☐ *Changing the initial thought*
- ☐ *Managing the emotion when it appears*
- ☐ *Choosing a different behavior*
- ☐ *Reframing the follow-up thought*

Explain your choice:

_____

_____

Step 3: Create Intervention Strategies

For each challenging loop, develop a plan to break the cycle:

Situation Description	Current Loop	Intervention Points	New Strategy

Here is an example for one strategy card:

- **Situation 1:** *Test Anxiety*
  - **What usually happens:** *Negative thoughts spiral before tests ("I'm going to fail" "I always mess up" "I'll never be good at this" increased anxiety poor focus worse performance)*
  - **Where I can intervene:** *When I catch the first "I'm going to fail" thought*
  - **New strategy to try:** *Pause and replace with "I've studied and I know what I know. This is just one test and I'll do my best."*
  - **Support I need:** *Reminders from friends/teachers that one test doesn't define me, and practice identifying these thoughts early*

Fill in your strategy cards:

Situation 1:

- *What usually happens:*_____
- *Where I can intervene:*_____
- *New strategy to try:*_____
- *Support I need:*_____

Situation 2:

- *What usually happens:*_____
- *Where I can intervene:*_____
- *New strategy to try:*_____
- *Support I need:*_____

Situation 3:

- *What usually happens:*_____
- *Where I can intervene:*_____
- *New strategy to try:*_____
- *Support I need:*_____

Situation 4:

- *What usually happens:*_____
- *Where I can intervene:*_____
- *New strategy to try:*_____
- *Support I need:*_____

Step 4: Practice Thought-Emotion Management

Choose one situation to focus on this week:

- **Triggering situation:**_____

- **Current thought pattern:**_____

- **Resulting emotion:**_____

- **New thought to try:**_____

- **Expected emotion shift:**_____

	Situation	Old thought/ emotion	New thought attempted	Result
Mon				
Tues				
Weds				
Thurs				
Fri				
Sat				
Sun				

Step 5: Build Your Response Library

Create quick responses for common thought triggers:

When I think "Nobody likes me":

- *Instead, I'll think:*_____
- *Because:*_____

When I think "I'm going to fail":

- *Instead, I'll think:*_____
- *Because:*_____

When I think "It's all my fault":

- *Instead, I'll think:*_____
- *Because:*_____

Pro Tip: *Think of your thoughts and emotions like a playlist - you can't always control what song comes on first, but you can choose what plays next. The more you practice managing this connection, the better you get at "changing the tune" when needed!*

Long-Term Emotion Management Plan

Purpose:

To create your personal emotion management strategy for the future, like designing a long-term health and fitness plan for your feelings.

Materials Needed:

- Pen or pencil
- Your experience from previous exercises
- Forward-thinking mindset

Real-Life Application

Sam struggled with emotional ups and downs until they created their long-term management plan. By identifying their emotional patterns throughout the school year (like higher anxiety during exams and mood dips during winter), they could prepare in advance. Having a plan made them feel more confident and in control, even during challenging times.

Step 1: Create Your Emotional Calendar

January

S	M	T	W	T	F	S
			1	2	3	4
5	6	7	8	9	10	11
12	13	14	15	16	17	18
19	20	21	22	23	24	25
26	27	28	29	30	31	

Example: Emotional Challenges:

Week 1: New Year's Resolutions

Week 2: Post-Holiday Blues

Week 3: Work Deadlines

Week 4: Winter Fatigue

Week 5: Planning for February

February

S	M	T	W	T	F	S
						1
2	3	4	5	6	7	8
9	10	11	12	13	14	15
16	17	18	19	20	21	22
23	24	25	26	27	28	

Emotional Challenges:

_____

_____

_____

_____

_____

March

S	M	T	W	T	F	S
						1
2	3	4	5	6	7	8
9	10	11	12	13	14	15
16	17	18	19	20	21	22
23	24	25	26	27	28	29
30	31					

Emotional Challenges:

_____

_____

_____

_____

_____

July

S	M	T	W	T	F	S
		1	2	3	4	5
6	7	8	9	10	11	12
13	14	15	16	17	18	19
20	21	22	23	24	25	26
27	28	29	30	31		

Emotional Challenges:

_____

_____

_____

_____

_____

August

S	M	T	W	T	F	S
					1	2
3	4	5	6	7	8	9
10	11	12	13	14	15	16
17	18	19	20	21	22	23
24	25	26	27	28	29	30
31						

Emotional Challenges:

_____

_____

_____

_____

_____

September

S	M	T	W	T	F	S
	1	2	3	4	5	6
7	8	9	10	11	12	13
14	15	16	17	18	19	20
21	22	23	24	25	26	27
28	29	30				

Emotional Challenges:

_____

_____

_____

_____

_____

October

S	M	T	W	T	F	S
			1	2	3	4
5	6	7	8	9	10	11
12	13	14	15	16	17	18
19	20	21	22	23	24	25
26	27	28	29	30	31	

Emotional Challenges:

_____
_____
_____
_____

November

S	M	T	W	T	F	S
						1
2	3	4	5	6	7	8
9	10	11	12	13	14	15
16	17	18	19	20	21	22
23	24	25	26	27	28	29
30						

Emotional Challenges:

_____
_____
_____
_____

December

S	M	T	W	T	F	S
	1	2	3	4	5	6
7	8	9	10	11	12	13
14	15	16	17	18	19	20
21	22	23	24	25	26	27
28	29	30	31			

Emotional Challenges:

_____
_____
_____
_____

Mark your calendar:

- ☐ *School stress periods*
- ☐ *Important social events*
- ☐ *Family situations*
- ☐ *Personal challenges*
- ☐ *Positive events to look forward to*

Step 2: Design Your Seasonal Strategies

*Different seasons often bring different emotional challenges.
Let's plan for each:*

Here is an example:

- **Fall (School Start):**
  - **Common Emotions:** Anxiety and excitement mixed together
  - **Challenges:** New classes, schedule changes, social pressure
  - **Prevention Strategies:** Preview my schedule the night before, find one friendly face in each class
  - **Support Needed:** Regular check-ins with my favorite teacher or counselor

Fall (School Start):

- *Common Emotions:*_____
- *Challenges:*_____
- *Prevention Strategies:*_____
- *Support Needed:*_____

Winter (Cold/Dark Season):

- *Common Emotions:*_____
- *Challenges:*_____
- *Prevention Strategies:*_____
- *Support Needed:*_____

Spring (Change/Testing):

- *Common Emotions:*_____
- *Challenges:*_____
- *Prevention Strategies:*_____
- *Support Needed:*_____

Summer (Transitions):

- *Common Emotions:*_____
- *Challenges:*_____
- *Prevention Strategies:*_____
- *Support Needed:*_____

Step 3: Create Your Maintenance Plan

Example Maintenance Plan:

Daily Practices
- ☐ *Morning routine: Take 3 deep breaths, rate mood 1-5 while brushing teeth*
- ☐ *Afternoon check-in: Text one positive thing to support buddy during lunch*
- ☐ *Evening wind-down: 5-minute journal: "Today was..." before bed*

Weekly Practices:
- ☐ *Emotion review: Sunday night: Circle 3 emojis that match my week*
- ☐☐ *Stress relief: Wednesday dance break to favorite song*
- ☐☐ *Connection time: Friday lunch with friend group*

Monthly Practices:
- ☐ *Progress check: First of month: Review journal highlights*
- ☐☐ *Strategy update: Pick one new coping skill to try*
- ☐☐ *Self-care focus: Choose theme (sleep, exercise, etc.)*

The key is making each task:
- *Takes less than 5 minutes*
- *Links to something you already do*
- *Feels doable even on hard days*

Now lets create your maintenance plan:

Daily Practices
- ☐ **Morning routine:**_____
- ☐ **Afternoon check-in:**_____
- ☐ **Evening wind-down:**_____

Daily Practices
- ☐ *Morning routine:* _____
- ☐ *Afternoon check-in:* _____
- ☐ *Evening wind-down:* _____

Weekly Practices:
- ☐ *Emotion review:* _____
- ☐ *Stress relief:* _____
- ☐ *Connection time:* _____

Monthly Practices:
- ☐ *Progress check:* _____
- ☐ *Strategy update:* _____
- ☐ *Self-care focus:* _____

Step 4: Build Your Growth Roadmap

Current emotional skills

Skills to develop

Timeline for practice

Milestone celebration

Current Emotional Strengths: Think about what your friends come to you for.

1._____
2._____
3._____

Skills to Develop: Think about moments that often trip you up.

1._____
2._____
3._____

<u>**Timeline for Practice:**</u>

- **Next Month:** *Pick ONE tiny new habit - something so small you could do it even on your worst day. What's your level 1?*

_____

- **3 Months:** *What's one way you could open up more? Choose something that feels a little scary but not terrifying.*

_____

- **6 Months:** *Pick a new skill you want to practice - like trying a calm-down strategy when you're already feeling okay (that's the best time to practice!)*

_____

- **1 Year:** *Imagine your best friend describing how you've grown. What would make you proud to hear them say?*

_____

- **Celebrate your Milestones:** *What will you do to celebrate once you develop each skill?*

_____

Step 5: Create Your Support System Directory

📞 Name   **📞 Role**

📞 Type of support they offer   **📞 Best way to reach**

Professional Support:

- *Name:*_____
- *Best way to reach:*_____
- *Type of support they offer:*_____

Friend Support:

- *Name:*_____
- *Best way to reach:*_____
- *Type of support they offer:*_____

Family Support:

- *Name:*_____
- *Best way to reach:*_____
- *Type of support they offer:*_____

Step 6: Develop Your Crisis Prevention Plan

Use skills you have learned throughout this chapter.

Early Warning Signs:

- *Physical:*_____

- *Emotional:*_____

- *Behavioral:*_____

Prevention Steps:

1._____

2._____

3._____

Emergency Contacts:

- *Immediate Help:*_____

- *Backup Support:*_____

- *Professional Care:*_____

Pro Tip: *Think of this plan like a weather app - it helps you prepare for emotional "weather" before it hits. The more detailed your plan, the better equipped you'll be to handle whatever comes your way!*

Chapter 3 Reflection

Take a moment to reflect on your emotional regulation journey:

My biggest emotional regulation breakthrough was:

_____

_____

_____

The strategy that helps me most is:

_____

_____

_____

I'm proud of myself for:

_____

_____

_____

My next emotional growth goal is:

_____

_____

Remember: *Managing emotions is a lifelong journey. You've now got advanced tools and strategies - be proud of how far you've come and excited about how much more you can grow!*

Social Intelligence Training

"The most important single ingredient in the formula of success is knowing how to get along with people."

- Theodore Roosevelt

▮▷ Understanding Social Intelligence

Think of social intelligence like having a superpower that helps you navigate all your relationships - from close friendships to casual conversations with classmates. It's about reading social situations, understanding others, and choosing how to respond in ways that work well for everyone involved.

Real-Life Application:

Jack always wondered why some people seemed to make friends so easily. After developing his social intelligence skills, he realized it wasn't magic - it was about paying attention to social cues, showing genuine interest in others, and responding thoughtfully. Soon he was able to turn casual conversations into real connections!

Why Advanced Regulation Matters

Having strong social intelligence is like having:

- *A decoder ring for body language and tone of voice*

- *A friendship-building toolkit*

- *An emotional bridge to connect with others*

- *A conflict resolution superpower*

- *A respect-earning ability*

Social Situation Scanner

Purpose:

To develop your ability to read and understand social situations, like having a high-tech scanner that helps you understand what's really happening in social interactions.

Materials Needed:

- Pen or pencil
- Your observation skills
- Willingness to analyze social situations

Real-Life Application

Maya used to feel lost in group conversations until she developed her "social scanner." She learned to notice when people were getting bored (checking phones), interested (leaning in), or wanting to speak (opening their mouths slightly). This helped her know when to change topics, ask questions, or give others a chance to talk.

Step 1: Calibrate Your Social Scanner

Let's identify what to look for in social situations. Check the signals you're already good at spotting:

Verbal Signals:
- ☐ *Tone of voice*
- ☐ *Word choice*
- ☐ *Speaking pace*
- ☐ *Volume level*
- ☐ *Pauses in speech*
- ☐ *Other:_____*

Body Language:
- ☐ *Facial expressions*
- ☐ *Body positioning*
- ☐ *Hand gestures*
- ☐ *Eye contact*
- ☐ *Personal space*
- ☐ *Other:_____*

Group Dynamics:
- ☐ *Who's talking most*
- ☐ *Who's being quiet*
- ☐ *Sub-groups forming*
- ☐ *Energy level*
- ☐ *Inclusion/exclusion*
- ☐ *Other:_____*

Step 2: Practice Your Scanning Skills

Choose a recent social situation to analyze:

Here is an example:

- **Scenario:** Lunch Movie Planning
- **People involved:** Three friends at lunch table

What I noticed:

Verbal signals:

- **Friend 1:** "Let's go to movies!"
- **Friend 2:** "Maybe... I'm busy"
- **Friend 3:** "Cool, which movie?"

Body language:

- **Friend 1:** Excited, big gestures
- **Friend 2:** Looking down, quiet
- **Friend 3:** Relaxed, leaning in

Group dynamics:

- Everyone follows excited friend's lead
- Quiet friend seems disconnected
- Others engaged but not noticing Friend 2

What these clues told me:

- Quiet friend might feel left out or uncomfortable
- Could help by checking in privately or suggesting different plans

Now lets create your own:

- *Scenario:* _____

- *People involved:* _____

What I noticed:

- **Verbal signals:**

  _____

  _____

- **Body language:**

  _____

  _____

- **Group dynamics:**

  _____

  _____

- **What these clues told me:**

  _____

  _____

Step 3: Create Your Social Signals Guide

Fill in your guide:

Here is an example:

- **Signal:** *Tight Lips*
- **Could mean:** *Disapproval, frustration, or holding back emotions.*
- **Best response:** *Address the situation gently by asking, "Is something on your mind?" or giving them space to open up when they're ready.*

Signal 1: *Crossed Arms*

Could mean:_____

Best response:
_____

Signal 2: *Avoiding Eye Contact*

Could mean:_____

Best response:
_____

Signal 3: *Leaning In*

Could mean:_____

Best response:
_____

Signal 4: *Leaning Away*

Could mean:_____

Best response:
_____

Signal 5: *Fidgeting*

Could mean:_____

Best response:
_____

Signal 6: *Smiling*

Could mean:_____

Best response:_____

Signal 7: *Looking at a Phone*

Could mean:_____

Best response:_____

Signal 8: *Raised Eyebrows*

Could mean:_____

Best response:_____

Signal 9: *Talking Quickly*

Could mean:_____

Best response:_____

Signal 10: *Mirroring Body Language*

Could mean:_____

Best response:_____

Step 4: Real-Time Scanning Practice

*Pick three different types of social situations to practice
your scanning this week:*

Situation 1: *(Example: Lunch table)*

What to watch for:_____

What I learned:_____

Situation 2: *(Example: Team practice)*

What to watch for:_____

What I learned:_____

Situation 3: *(Example: Family dinner)*

What to watch for:_____

What I learned:_____

Weekly Observation Log:

	Day 1	Day 2	Day 3	Day 4	Day 5	Day 6	Day 7
Time:							
Setting:							
Signals Noticed:							
Interpretations:							
What Worked or What Didn't Work:							

__Pro Tip:__ Remember, social scanning isn't about judging - it's about understanding! Think of yourself as a friendly scientist studying how people connect and communicate.

Communication Style Laboratory

Purpose:

To experiment with different ways of communicating and find what works best in different situations, like having a lab where you can test and perfect your communication formulas.

Materials Needed:

- Pen or pencil
- Willingness to try new approaches
- Open mind to feedback

Real-Life Application

Riley always defaulted to being super direct, which sometimes came across as harsh. In their communication lab work, they discovered they could be honest while still being tactful. Instead of saying "That's a terrible idea," they learned to say "I have some concerns about that approach. Could we explore other options?" The result? People were more receptive to their input!

Step 1: Identify Your Current Communication Style

Rate how often you use each style (1 = rarely, 5 = very often):

Passive:

(Going along with others, avoiding conflict)

☐ 1 ☐ 2 ☐ 3 ☐ 4 ☐ 5

Aggressive:

(Forceful, putting your needs first)

☐ 1 ☐ 2 ☐ 3 ☐ 4 ☐ 5

Passive-Aggressive:

(Indirect resistance, hidden anger)

☐ 1 ☐ 2 ☐ 3 ☐ 4 ☐ 5

Assertive:

(Clear, respectful, balanced)

☐ 1 ☐ 2 ☐ 3 ☐ 4 ☐ 5

Step 2: Communication Style Experiments

Let's test different approaches, choose a style type that fits best from step 1 *(how do you usually act?)*:

- **Experiment 1:** *Speaking Up in Class*
- **Current style:**_____
- **New approach to try:**_____
- **What happened:**_____
- **What I learned:**_____

- **Experiment 2:** *Disagreeing with Friends*
- **Current style:**_____
- **New approach to try:**_____
- **What happened:**_____
- **What I learned:**_____

- **Experiment 3:** *Making Requests*
- **Current style:**_____
- **New approach to try:**_____
- **What happened:**_____
- **What I learned:**_____

- **Experiment 4:** *Managing Stress Before a Test*
- **Current style:**_____
- **New approach to try:**_____
- **What happened:**_____
- **What I learned:**_____

Step 3: Build Your Communication Formula Lab

Create your go-to phrases for different situations:

- **When you need to say no:**_____
- **Instead of:** *"I can't" or "Whatever..."*_____
- **Try this:**
  _____

- **When you disagree:**_____
- **Instead of:** *"You're wrong" or staying silent*_____
- **Try this:**_____

- **When you need help:**_____
- **Instead of:** *"Never mind" or demanding*_____
- **Try this:**_____

- **When you're upset:**_____
- **Instead of:** *"I'm fine" or exploding*_____
- **Try this:**_____

Step 4: Design Your Communication Toolkit

Fill in your favorite tools:

First example for each is provided

- **Conversation Starters:**

    1. *"I'd love to hear your thoughts on [topic]."*_____

    2._____

    3._____

- **Active Listening Responses:**

    1. *"I hear you, that must have been tough."*_____

    2._____

    3._____

- **Boundary Setting Phrases:**
    1. "I'm not comfortable continuing this conversation in that direction."
    2. _____
    3. _____

- **Conflict Resolution Approaches:**
    1. "Let's focus on finding a solution that works for both of us."
    2. _____
    3. _____

- **Exit Strategies:**
    - *These are useful for ending a conversation politely or defusing an uncomfortable situation.*

    1. "I think we've both shared our thoughts. Let's revisit this later."
    2. _____
    3. _____

- **Conflict Resolution Approaches:**
    1. "Let's focus on finding a solution that works for both of us."
    2. _____
    3. _____

- **Recovery Phrases**
    - *These help recover from any awkward moments or misunderstandings during a conversation.*

1. *"That didn't come out how I intended–let me rephrase."*
2. _____
3. _____

Step 5: Practice Scenarios
Try these common situations:

- **Scenario 1:** *Friend Pressure*
- **Challenge:** *A friend wants you to skip studying for a hangout*
- **Current response:**_____
- **New approach:**_____
- **How it felt:**_____

- **Scenario 2:** *Social Media Drama*
- **Challenge:** *You're being tagged in posts by friends you don't get along with, and it's making you uncomfortable*
- **Current response:**_____
- **New approach:**_____
- **How it felt:**_____

- **Scenario 3:** *Peer Comparison*
- **Challenge:** *A classmate makes you feel bad by constantly comparing your grades to theirs*
- **Current response:**_____
- **New approach:**_____
- **How it felt:**_____

- **Scenario 5**: *Group Project Stress*
- **Challenge**: *You're stuck doing all the work for a group project because your teammates aren't contributing*
- **Current response:**_____
- **New approach:**_____
- **How it felt:**_____

- **Scenario 6**: *Unwanted Advice*
- **Challenge**: *An older sibling or relative keeps giving you advice about how to handle your friendships*
- **Current response:**_____
- **New approach:**_____
- **How it felt:**_____

Step 6: Communication Style Journal

Track your communication experiments this week:

Track your communication experiments this week:

Monday

Situation	Style used	Effectiveness rating	Notes for improvement

Tuesday

Situation	Style used	Effectiveness rating	Notes for improvement

Wednesday

Situation	Style used	Effectiveness rating	Notes for improvement

Thursday

Situation	Style used	Effectiveness rating	Notes for improvement

Friday

Situation	Style used	Effectiveness rating	Notes for improvement

Saturday

Situation	Style used	Effectiveness rating	Notes for improvement

Sunday

Situation	Style used	Effectiveness rating	Notes for improvement

Pro Tip: *Think of communication styles like different apps on your phone - each one has its perfect use case. The trick isn't using one style all the time, but knowing which style works best in each situation!*

Relationship Building Workshop

Purpose:

To develop skills for creating and maintaining healthy relationships of all types, like being an architect designing strong bridges between people.

Materials Needed:

- Pen or pencil
- Your relationship experiences
- Willingness to build connections

Real-Life Application

Aisha was great at making first connections but struggled to develop deeper friendships. Through relationship building practice, she learned that strong relationships need regular "maintenance" - like checking in with friends regularly, remembering important details about their lives, and being there during both good and tough times. Her friendships grew stronger when she started treating them like plants that needed regular care!

Step 1: Map Your Relationship Circles

Place your current relationships on the map:

Inner Circle (Closest Relationships):

_____

Close Friends/Family:

_____

Friends/Regular Contacts:

_____

Acquaintances:

_____

Step 2: Relationship Building Blocks

Rate your strength in each area (1 = needs work, 5 = very strong):

- **Trust Building:**_____
  - ☐ 1 ☐ 2 ☐ 3 ☐ 4 ☐ 5
- **My best trust-building strategy:**_____

- **Active Listening:**_____
  - ☐ 1 ☐ 2 ☐ 3 ☐ 4 ☐ 5
- **My best listening technique:**_____

- **Showing Support:**_____
  - ☐ 1 ☐ 2 ☐ 3 ☐ 4 ☐ 5
- **My best way to show support:**_____

- **Setting Boundaries:**_____
  - ☐ 1 ☐ 2 ☐ 3 ☐ 4 ☐ 5
- **My best boundary-setting phrase:**_____

Step 3: Create Your Connection Strategies

Rate your strength in each area (1 = needs work, 5 = very strong):

For New Relationships:

- *(Like planting a seed)*

First Connection:

- *What I'll say:*_____
- *What I'll ask:*_____
- *How I'll follow up:*_____

Building Trust:

- *Small steps to take:*_____
- *Things to share:*_____
- *Ways to be reliable:*_____

For Existing Relationships:

- *(Like tending a garden)*

Strengthening Bonds:

- *Regular check-ins:*_____
- *Shared activities:*_____
- *Ways to show care:*_____

Step 4: Relationship Repair Kit

Rate your strength in each area (1 = needs work, 5 = very strong):

- **When Trust is Broken:**

Step 1: *Acknowledge the breach of trust and express your feelings.*

How did you feel when trust was broken in your relationship? **Write it here:**

_____

_____

Step 2: *Have an open conversation to understand what happened and why trust was broken. Think about a time when trust was broken. What could you say to start a conversation?* **Write it here:**

_____

_____

Step 3: *Work on rebuilding trust through consistent actions and communication. How can you take actions to rebuild trust?* **Write some ideas:**

_____

_____

- **When Distance Grows:**

Step 1: *Acknowledge the distance and discuss the reasons behind it.*

When you notice distance growing, how can you address it? **Write it here:**

_____

_____

Step 2: *Reconnect by sharing your feelings and making time for each other. What would you say to reconnect with someone when the distance has grown?* **Write it here:**

_____

_____

Step 3: Create new habits or traditions to strengthen the relationship and close the gap. What could you do to strengthen your relationship and bring it closer together?

_____

_____

- **When Boundaries Are Crossed:**

Step 1: Address the boundary violation calmly and respectfully.
When someone crosses a boundary, how can you calmly address it? **Write it here:** _____

_____

Step 2: Set clear boundaries moving forward and explain their importance. What boundaries are important to you, and how can you clearly communicate them?

_____

_____

Step 3: Take responsibility for your own boundaries and work together to ensure they are respected. How can you make sure your boundaries are respected, and how can you help others respect theirs?

_____

_____

Personal Examples:
Now, let's think about some personal examples and how these steps could help in real situations.

- **When Trust Was Broken:**

Have you ever had trust broken in a relationship? What was the situation, and how did you address it?

_____

_____

- **When Distance Grew:**

Has there ever been a time when you felt distant from someone? How did you try to close that gap?

_____

_____

Step 5: Design Your Relationship Goals

Rate your strength in each area (1 = needs work, 5 = very strong):

Short-term Goals (Next month):

1. Make one new connection

- *Action steps:*_____

2. Strengthen one existing relationship

- *Action steps:*_____

3. Repair one stressed relationship

- *Action steps:*_____

Step 6: My Connection Map

Quick Daily Check-ins: *Pick 1-2 people to connect with each day, write their names:*

Morning buddy:_____ *(who helps start your day?)*

Afternoon chat:_____ *(lunch friend?)*

Evening check:_____ *(family/close friend?)*

Weekly Hangouts: *Choose what works with your schedule:*

Definite plans:_____ *(like "Tuesday lunch with Sam")*

Flex time:_____ *(like "weekend gaming")*

Group stuff:_____ *(like "study group")*

Pro Tip: *Think of relationships like plants in a garden - some need daily attention, others weekly or monthly, but they all need regular care to stay healthy and grow. The key is finding the right balance of attention for each relationship in your life!*

Conflict Resolution Training

Purpose:

To develop skills for handling disagreements and conflicts effectively, like becoming a peace negotiator for your own life.

Materials Needed:

- Pen or pencil
- Open mind for new approaches
- Willingness to find solutions

Real-Life Application

Marcus used to either avoid conflicts completely or get defensive and argue. Through conflict resolution training, he learned to stay calm and use a problem-solving approach. When his friend was upset about not being invited to hang out, instead of getting defensive (*"Well, you never invite me either!"*), he listened to their feelings and worked together to find a solution. The result? A stronger friendship

Step 1: Identify Your Conflict Style

How do you usually handle conflicts? Check your typical responses:

When faced with conflict, I tend to:

- ☐ *Avoid it completely*
- ☐ *Give in to keep peace*
- ☐ *Fight to win*
- ☐ *Look for compromise*
- ☐ *Try to solve the problem*
- ☐ *Other:* _____

Rate how well your current style works:

Not at all ☐ **1** ☐ **2** ☐ **3** ☐ **4** ☐ **5 Very well**

Step 2: Build Your Conflict Resolution Toolkit

<u>Tool Card 1:</u> *Cooling Down*

When to Use:

- *When emotions are running high and you or someone else need a moment to calm down before continuing a conversation.*

<u>Example:</u>

- ***Current Response:*** *"I just can't deal with this right now!"*
- ***New Approach:*** *"I think I need a break to cool down before we continue talking."*
- ***How it Felt:*** *"I felt calmer and more in control after taking a short break."*

Tool Card 2: *Active Listening*

When to Use:

- *When someone is talking to you about their feelings or thoughts, and you want to show you're really listening and understanding them.*

Example:

- *Current Response:*_____
- *New Approach:*_____
- *How it Felt:*_____

Tool Card 3: *Problem Solving*

When to Use:

- *When there's an issue that needs to be worked through or resolved in a way that benefits everyone involved.*

Example:

- *Current Response:*_____
- *New Approach:*_____
- *How it Felt:*_____

Tool Card 4: *Apologizing*

When to Use:

- *When there's an issue that needs to be worked through or resolved in a way that benefits everyone involved.*

Example:

- *Current Response:*_____
- *New Approach:*_____
- *How it Felt:*_____

<u>**Tool Card 5:**</u> *Setting Boundaries*

When to Use:

- *When someone is talking to you about their feelings or thoughts, and you want to show you're really listening and understanding them.*

Example:

- *Current Response:*_____
- *New Approach:*_____
- *How it Felt:*_____

<u>**Tool Card 6:**</u> *Expressing Feelings*

When to Use:

- *When there's an issue that needs to be worked through or resolved in a way that benefits everyone involved.*

Example:

- *Current Response:*_____
- *New Approach:*_____
- *How it Felt:*_____

Step 3: Practice Conflict Scenarios

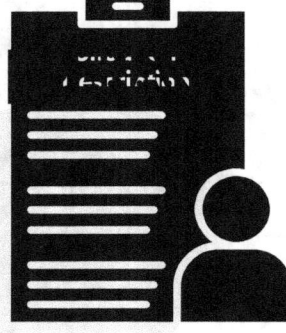
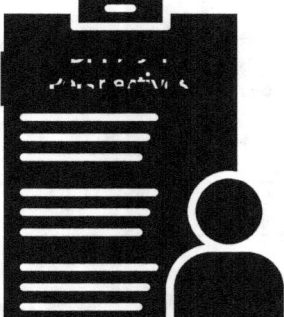

Possible Solutions

Scenario 1: *Friend Group Drama*

- Situation:_____
- Your perspective:_____
- Their perspective:_____
- Possible solutions:_____

Scenario 2: *Family Disagreement*

- Situation:_____
- Your perspective:_____
- Their perspective:_____
- Possible solutions:_____

Scenario 3: *School/Team Conflict*

- Situation:_____
- Your perspective:_____
- Their perspective:_____
- Possible solutions:_____

Step 4: Create Your Conflict Response Plan
Step-by-Step Guide:

1. First Response:
When conflict starts, I will:

_____

Instead of:

_____

2. Cooling Period:

My best cooling strategies:

- ☐ *Take deep breaths*
- ☐ *Count to ten*
- ☐ *Step away briefly*
- ☐ *Other:* _____

3. Understanding Phase:

Questions to ask:

- **What's their perspective?** _____
- **What are they feeling?** _____
- **What do they need?** _____

4. Solution Finding:

Brainstorm options:

1. _____
2. _____
3. _____

5. Agreement Making:

How to reach compromise:

_____

How to check everyone's okay with solution:

_____

Step 5: Create Your Conflict Prevention System
Prevention Checklist

Warning Signs to Watch For:

Check off any early warning signs you notice in your relationships.

- ☐ Rising tension
- ☐ Communication breakdown
- ☐ Repeated small issues
- ☐ Withdrawal or silence
- ☐ Increased frustration or irritability
- ☐ Avoiding difficult conversations
- ☐ Other: _____

Prevention Strategies:

Take steps to address these warning signs before they grow into bigger problems.

- ☐ **Regular check-ins:** Schedule times to check in with each other to discuss feelings and address any concerns.
- ☐ **Clear communication:** Practice speaking honestly and openly about your thoughts and emotions.
- ☐ **Boundary setting:** Make sure to clearly communicate personal boundaries and respect each other's limits.
- ☐ **Active listening:** Pay attention when the other person is speaking and show understanding.
- ☐ **Spending quality time together:** Make time to bond and enjoy each other's company to strengthen your connection.
- ☐ **Problem-solving together:** Work as a team to solve issues before they escalate.
- ☐ **Other:** _____

Communication Tips:

Use these tips to foster healthy communication and prevent misunderstandings.

- ☐ Use "I" statements: *Express your feelings without blaming others (e.g., "I feel hurt when...").*
- ☐ **Be open to feedback:** *Listen and stay open to what the other person is sharing.*
- ☐ **Stay calm:** *Take deep breaths if you feel overwhelmed, and avoid raising your voice.*
- ☐ **Focus on the issue, not the person:** *Address the behavior or situation, not the other person's character.*
- ☐ **Check for understanding:** *Repeat what the other person said to make sure you understand their point of view.*
- ☐ **Take breaks when needed:** *If emotions are high, it's okay to take a short break and come back to the conversation later.*
- ☐ *Other:* _____

Personal Example Section:

Reflect on a time when you noticed any of these warning signs. What did you do to prevent the situation from escalating?

- Warning Signs Noticed:_____
- Action Taken:_____
- How It Helped:_____

Step 6: Design Your Recovery Plan

After a conflict, I will:

_____

Check in with myself:

_____

Reflect on what I learned:

_____

Make amends if needed:

_____

Plan for the future:

_____

Pro Tip: _Think of conflict resolution like being a referee in a game - your job isn't to pick sides or declare winners, but to help everyone play fairly and find solutions that work for the whole team!_

Empathy Development

Purpose:

To strengthen your ability to understand and share the feelings of others, like developing an emotional GPS that helps you navigate other people's experiences.

Materials Needed:

- Pen or pencil
- Your observation skills
- Open heart and mind

Real-Life Application

Jamie never understood why their younger sibling got so upset over seemingly small things - until they practiced empathy. By imagining what it felt like to be younger, smaller, and often feeling powerless, Jamie started responding with more understanding. Instead of saying "Stop being a baby," they'd say "That seems really frustrating. Want to talk about it?" Their relationship improved dramatically!

Step 1: Empathy Self-Check

Rate your current empathy skills (1 = needs work, 5 = very strong):

Understanding others' feelings:

☐ 1 ☐ 2 ☐ 3 ☐ 4 ☐ 5

Seeing different perspectives:

☐ 1 ☐ 2 ☐ 3 ☐ 4 ☐ 5

Showing compassion:

☐ 1 ☐ 2 ☐ 3 ☐ 4 ☐ 5

Responding supportively:

☐ 1 ☐ 2 ☐ 3 ☐ 4 ☐ 5

Step 2: Perspective-Taking Practice

Card 1: New Student Situation: *There's a new student who keeps to themselves at lunch. Your perspective might be: "They're unfriendly or think they're too good for us." Try their perspective: "I'm nervous, don't know anyone, and afraid of being rejected." What you might not consider: Language barriers, previous bullying experiences, cultural differences Response plan: "Hi, would you like to sit with us? I remember being new last year..."*

Card 2: Friend Cancels Plans Situation: *Your best friend cancels movie plans last minute. Your perspective might be: "They don't value my time" or "They found something better to do." Try their perspective: "I'm overwhelmed with family obligations I can't control." What you might not consider: Family rules, responsibilities, personal struggles Response plan: "Everything okay? I'm disappointed but want to understand what's going on."*

Card 3: **Parent Sets Early Curfew Situation:** *Your parent insists on an earlier curfew than your friends have. Your perspective might be: "They don't trust me" or "They're trying to ruin my social life." Try their perspective: "I'm worried about their safety and doing my best to protect them." What you might not consider: Past experiences, neighborhood safety, family values Response plan: "Can we talk about what worries you and maybe find a compromise?"*

Card 4: **Teacher Assigns Extra Work Situation:** *Your teacher assigns homework over a holiday weekend. Your perspective might be: "They're unfair and don't care about our free time." Try their perspective: "I'm trying to keep the class on schedule for important exams." What you might not consider: Curriculum requirements, teaching responsibilities, trying to help students succeed Response plan: "Could you help me understand the purpose of this assignment?"*

Card 5: **Sibling Takes Your Things Situation:** *Your sibling borrowed your stuff without asking again. Your perspective might be: "They're disrespectful and don't care about my boundaries." Try their perspective: "I look up to my sibling and want to be like them." What you might not consider: Age differences, admiration, not understanding boundaries Response plan: "I know you like my things. Let's set up a way you can borrow them properly."*

Card 6: **Friend Seems Distant Situation:** *A close friend suddenly starts giving short responses to texts. Your perspective might be: "They're mad at me" or "They're being rude." Try their perspective: "I'm dealing with personal issues I'm not ready to share." What you might not consider: Mental health struggles, family problems, feeling overwhelmed Response plan: "I've noticed you seem different lately. I'm here if you want to talk."*

Choose a recent situation:

- *What happened:*_____
- *From my perspective:*_____
- *From their perspective:*_____
- *What I didn't consider:*_____
- *How this changes things:*_____

Step 3: Emotion Recognition Training

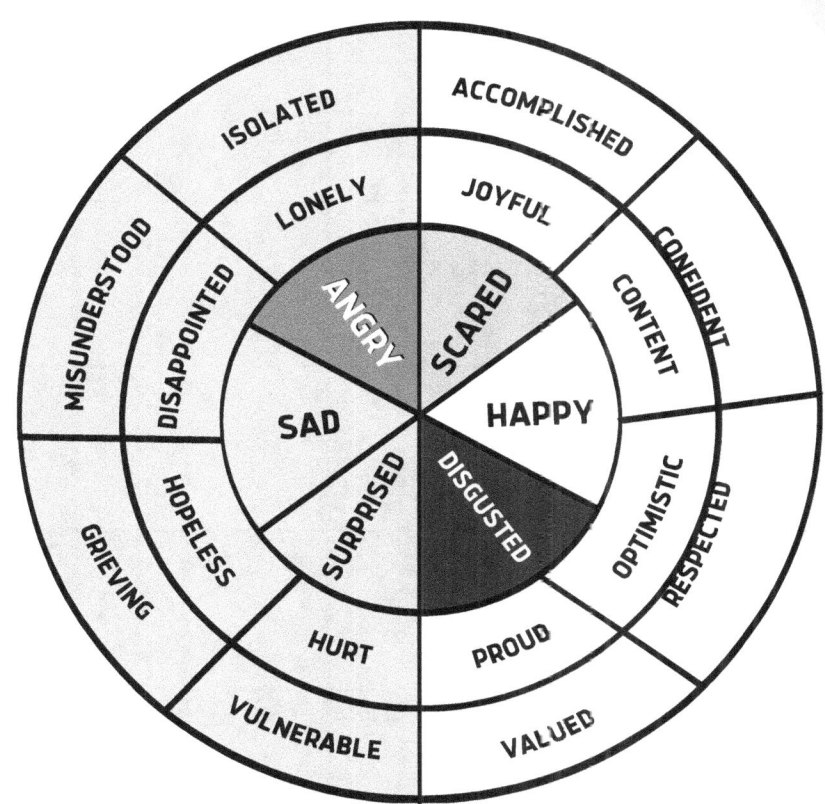

Practice identifying emotions:

- *In others' facial expressions:*

  _____

- *In tone of voice:*

  _____

- *In body language:*

  _____

- *In what's not being said:*

  _____

Step 4: Build Your Empathy Response Library

Instead of: "Get over it"

*Try:*_____

Instead of: "That's not a big deal"

*Try:*_____

Instead of: "Why are you so upset?"

*Try:*_____

Instead of: "At least..."

*Try:*_____

Step 5: Real-World Empathy Practice

Daily Empathy Challenges:

1. Notice someone's mood:

- *Who:*_____
- *What I observed:*_____
- *How I responded:*_____

2. Ask about someone's experience:

- *Who:*_____
- *What I learned:*_____
- *How it changed my view:*_____

3. Offer support:

- *Who:*_____
- *What they needed:*_____
- *How I helped:*_____

Step 6: Create Your Empathy-Building Plan

Weekly Practice Plan:

Monday: Notice & Name

- *Morning:* Notice three people's facial expressions during first class
- *Afternoon:* Identify two classmates' moods by their body language
- *Evening:* Name three emotions you saw in family members Reflection Space: What surprised you about what you noticed?

Tuesday: Listen & Learn

- *Morning:* Practice not interrupting in conversations
- *Afternoon:* Ask follow-up questions in at least two chats
- *Evening:* Give full attention to someone sharing a story Reflection Space: What did you learn by listening more carefully?

Wednesday: Walk in Their Shoes

- *Morning:* Consider a teacher's perspective about late assignments
- *Afternoon:* Think about why a friend acted differently than usual
- *Evening:* Imagine a sibling's view in a family situation Reflection Space: How did seeing other perspectives change your reactions?

Thursday: Connect & Care

- *Morning:* Ask someone how they're really doing
- *Afternoon:* Offer help to someone who seems stressed

- **Evening:** *Show understanding for someone's feelings Reflection Space: How did others respond to your care?*

Friday: Stretch Your Empathy
- **Morning:** *Notice three people's facial expressions during first class*
- **Afternoon:** *Identify two classmates' moods by their body language*
- **Evening:** *Name three emotions you saw in family members Reflection Space: What surprised you about what you noticed?*

Weekend: Review & Reflect
- *What worked well this week?*
- *What situations were challenging?*
- *What will you try differently next week? **Reflection Space:***

_____

Progress Tracking Chart: [ ] = Did it [ ] = Partially did it [X] = Didn't do it

Activity	Mon	Tues	Weds	Thurs	Fri	Sat	Sun
Notice & Name							
Listen & Learn							
Walk in Shoes							
Connect & Care							
Stretch Empathy							

Weekly Goals:

- **Monday:** *Notice others' feelings*
- **Tuesday:** *Practice active listening*
- **Wednesday:** *Show understanding*
- **Thursday:** *Offer support*
- **Friday:** *See new perspectives*
- **Weekend:** *Reflect and connect*

Track Your Progress:

- *What's getting easier:*
- *What's still challenging:*
- *New insights gained:*

Pro Tip: *Think of empathy like a superpower that lets you see the world through others' eyes. The more you practice, the stronger this power becomes!*

Notes for especially challenging situations:

- ☐ *When someone's very different from you*
- ☐ *When you're upset yourself*
- ☐ *When you disagree strongly*
- ☐ *When you don't understand their reaction*

Your strategies for these times:

_____

_____

_____

Pro Tip: Remember, being empathetic doesn't mean you have to agree with everyone - it just means you're trying to understand their experience. It's like being a good translator between different emotional languages!

Social Skills Integration

Purpose:

To combine and apply all your social intelligence skills in real-life situations, like becoming a master chess player who can use different strategies together to succeed.

Materials Needed:

- Pen or pencil
- Your social skills toolkit
- Willingness to practice combined skills

Real-Life Application

Sophia used to handle each social situation with just one skill at a time - either just listening, or just showing empathy, or just using clear communication. When she learned to combine skills, her social interactions improved dramatically. During a friend group conflict, she used her scanning skills to read the room, empathy to understand each person's perspective, communication skills to express her thoughts clearly, and conflict resolution skills to help find a solution. It was like conducting an orchestra where all the instruments played together!

Step 1: Create Your Skills Master List

Let's take inventory of all the social skills you've learned and practiced. This will help you see what tools you have available to use in different situations.

First, go through each skill category below. **For each specific skill:**

1. *Check the box if you've learned this skill*
2. *Rate how comfortable you are using it (1-5)*
3. *Write a real example of how you've used it or could use it*
4. *Note any challenges you have with this skill*

Communication Skills Section:

Active Listening:
- *I know this skill* ☐
- *Comfort level:* ☐ 1 ☐ 2 ☐ 3 ☐ 4 ☐ 5
- *My example of using this:*

_____
- *My biggest challenge with this:*

_____

Clear Expression:
- *I know this skill* ☐
- *Comfort level:* ☐ 1 ☐ 2 ☐ 3 ☐ 4 ☐ 5
- *My example of using this:*

_____
- *My biggest challenge with this:*

_____

Body Language:
- *I know this skill* ☐
- *Comfort level:* ☐ 1 ☐ 2 ☐ 3 ☐ 4 ☐ 5

- *My example of using this:*

_____

- *My biggest challenge with this:*

_____

Reading People Skills Section:

Emotion Recognition:
- *I know this skill* ☐
- *Comfort level:* ☐ 1 ☐ 2 ☐ 3 ☐ 4 ☐ 5
- *My example of using this:*

_____

- *My biggest challenge with this:*

_____

Social Cues Detection:
- *I know this skill* ☐
- *Comfort level:* ☐ 1 ☐ 2 ☐ 3 ☐ 4 ☐ 5
- *My example of using this:*

_____

- *My biggest challenge with this:*

_____

Relationship Skills Section:

Trust Building:
- *I know this skill* ☐
- *Comfort level:* ☐ 1 ☐ 2 ☐ 3 ☐ 4 ☐ 5
- *My example of using this:*

_____

- *My biggest challenge with this:*

_____

Now look at your completed inventory and answer:

My strongest skills are:

1._____

2._____

3._____

Skills I want to improve:

1._____

2._____

3._____

Skills I use most often:

1._____

2._____

3._____

Pro Tip: Keep this inventory handy! When you face a social situation, you can look back at it like checking your toolbox before starting a project.

Step 2: Situation-Based Integration Practice

In this step, you'll practice combining different social skills together in real situations you might face. Think of it like being a chef who knows how to combine different ingredients to make a great meal!

Complex Scenario 1: Group Project Drama

Let's walk through exactly how to handle this situation step by step.

A. First, analyze the situation: Write down who's involved in your group:

_____

What's each person's usual working style?
- *Person 1:* _____
- *Person 2:* _____
- *Person 3:* _____

Any past conflicts or issues to consider?

_____

B. Create your action plan:

Phase 1 (First Meeting):
- *Check the skills you'll use:*
    - ○ ☐ *Reading body language to gauge everyone's mood*
    - ○ ☐ *Active listening to understand everyone's ideas*
    - ○ ☐ *Clear communication to establish group expectations*
- *Write your opening lines: "Hi everyone, I was thinking we could..."*

_____

How will you include everyone?

_____

Phase 2 (Working Together): Create your communication system:
- *How you'll share updates:* _____
    - ○ ☐ *How often you'll check in:* _____
    - ○ ☐ *How you'll divide work:* _____
- *Write down potential problems and solutions:*

Problem:

Someone isn't doing their share I'll say: _____

And then: _____

Problem:

Two people disagree on approach I'll say: _____

And then: _____

Phase 3 (Handling Challenges): Create your backup plans:
- *If someone misses deadlines:*

_____

_____

- *If conflicts arise:*

_____

_____

Complex Scenario 2: New Social Circle

A. Pre-Integration Research: Observe the group for one week and note:
- *Their typical meeting spots:*

_____

- *Common interests they share:*

_____

- *Group dynamics (who talks to who):*

_____

B. Create Your Integration Timeline:
- **Week 1 Actions: Monday:**_____

  (Example: Sit near group at lunch, observe conversations)
- **Tuesday:**_____

  (Example: Make one positive comment in group discussion)
- **Wednesday:**_____

  (Example: Ask question about shared interest)
- **Thursday:**_____

  (Example: Share relevant story or experience)
- **Friday:**_____

  (Example: Suggest weekend activity)

C. Track Your Progress:

- *Each day, note: What worked:_____ What felt awkward:_____ What to try tomorrow:_____*
- *Month 1 Goals: Social connections to make:*

_____

_____

Activities to join:

_____

_____

D. Rate Your Comfort Level Each Week:

- *Week 1:* ☐ 1 ☐ 2 ☐ 3 ☐ 4 ☐ 5
- *Week 2:* ☐ 1 ☐ 2 ☐ 3 ☐ 4 ☐ 5
- *Week 3:* ☐ 1 ☐ 2 ☐ 3 ☐ 4 ☐ 5
- *Week 4:* ☐ 1 ☐ 2 ☐ 3 ☐ 4 ☐ 5

Pro Tip: *Remember, integration takes time!*
It's okay to start small and build up gradually.

Step 3: Create Your Social Situations Playbook

In this step, you'll create your own guide for handling common social situations. Think of it like writing your own video game strategy guide!

A. Joining an Existing Conversation

1. First, observe the conversation:

- *Check what you notice:*
  - ☐ *How many people are talking*
  - ☐ *Their body language*

- ○ ☐ *The topic being discussed*
- ○ ☐ *The energy level (quiet/excited)*

2. Plan your entry:

- *Choose your approach (check one):*
  - ○ ☐ *Ask a question about the topic*
  - ○ ☐ *Share a relevant experience*
  - ○ ☐ *Give a compliment related to discussion*
  - ○ ☐ *Other:*_____

- **Write three possible opening lines:**

  1._____

  2._____

  3._____

3. Practice active participation:

- *Ways I can show I'm listening:*
  - ○ ☐ *Nodding*
  - ○ ☐ *Making eye contact*
  - ○ ☐ *Small verbal responses ("mm-hmm", "right")*
  - ○ ☐ *Other:*_____

Questions I could ask to keep conversation going:

  1._____

  2._____

  3._____

B. Supporting an Upset Friend

1. Notice distress signals:

- *What signs tell you they're upset?*

- *Physical signs:*_____
- *Voice tone:*_____
- *Words used:*_____
- *Behavior changes:*_____

2. Create your support sequence:
- *Start with observation:*
- *"I noticed that..."* (write 3 ways to say this)
  - 1._____
  - 2._____
  - 3._____

- **Show you care:**
- *"I care because..."* (write 3 ways to say this)
  - 1._____
  - 2._____
  - 3._____

- **Offer specific help:**
- *"Would it help if..."* (write 3 offers)
  - 1._____
  - 2._____
  - 3._____

C. Navigating Group Disagreement

1. Create your peace-keeper toolkit:
- *Calming phrases to use:*
- *When tensions rise:*

_____

- When someone's angry:

_____

- When people aren't listening:

_____

2. Make your mediation plan:

- **Step 1: Stop escalation**
  - Write your "pause button" phrases:

    _____

    _____

- **Step 2: Understand each side**
  - Questions to ask Person A:

    _____

    _____

  - Questions to ask Person B:

    _____

    _____

- **Step 3: Find common ground**
  - Look for shared interests:

    _____

    _____

- **Step 4: Suggest solutions**
  - Template for proposing compromise:
    - "What if we..."_____
    - "Could we try..."_____
    - "How about if..."_____

3. Practice Your Responses:

- When someone says: "That's stupid!"
  - I'll say:

_____

Pro Tips for Your Playbook:
- *Write notes about what works in different situations*
- *Add new strategies as you learn them*
- *Keep track of which approaches work best with different people*

Your Personal Notes Section:
- *Strategies that work best for me:*

_____

_____

- *Things to avoid:*

_____

_____

- *People who help me practice:*

_____

_____

Step 4: Advanced Integration Challenges

Let's create your weekly practice plan! Think of this like a workout schedule for your social skills - you'll start with basics and work up to more challenging exercises.

Monday: *Conversation Expansion Challenge*
- **Morning Challenge:**
  - *Choose one:*
    - ☐ *Say hello to someone new*
    - ☐ *Ask about someone's weekend*
    - ☐ *Give a genuine compliment*

- **Write what happened:**
  - *Who I talked to:*_____
  - *What I said:*_____
  - *Their response:*_____
  - *How it felt:*_____

- **Afternoon Challenge:**
  - *Pick a conversation to expand:*
    - *Setting:*_____
    - *Topic:*_____

- **Questions I asked to keep it going:**
  - *1._____*
  - *2._____*
  - *3._____*

- **Evening Reflection:**
  - *What worked well:*_____
  - *What I'll try tomorrow:*_____

Tuesday: *Emotional Support Challenge*

1. Notice and Name Emotions
  - *Watch three people and write down:*
    - *Person 1:_____ Emotion: _____*
    - *Person 2:_____ Emotion: _____*
    - *Person 3:_____ Emotion: _____*

2. Choose Someone to Support
  - *Who needs support today:*_____
  - *Signs I noticed:*_____

- **My support plan:**
  - *Step 1:*_____
  - *Step 2:*_____
  - *Step 3:*_____

- **3. Track Your Impact**
  - *How they responded:*_____
  - *What I learned:*_____

Wednesday: *Group Navigation Challenge*

- **1. Map Your Group Situation**
  - *Group activity chosen:*_____
  - *People involved:*_____
  - *My usual role:*_____

- **2. Try New Group Behaviors**
  - *Choose one to try:*
    - *Include someone quiet*
    - *Mediate a disagreement*
    - *Lead an activity*
    - *Bridge two sub-groups*

- **Document your experience:**
  - *What I did:*_____
  - *How others reacted:*_____
  - *What I learned:*_____

- **3. Advanced Group Skills**
  - *Choose a group challenge:*
    - ☐ *Help resolve conflict*
    - ☐ *Integrate new member*
    - ☐ *Improve group dynamics*

- **Write your strategy:**
  - *Step 1:*_____
  - *Step 2:*_____
  - *Step 3:*_____

Thursday: *Relationship Building Challenge*

- **1. Choose Your Focus**
  - *Pick one:*
    - ☐ Strengthen existing friendship
    - ☐ Build new connection
    - ☐ Repair strained relationship

- **2. Create Your Action Plan**
  - *Goal:*_____

- **Three steps to take:**
  - 1._____
  - 2._____
  - 3._____

- **3. Track Progress**
  - *Actions taken:*_____
  - *Results:*_____
  - *Next steps:*_____

Friday: *Social Problem Solving Challenge*

- **1. Identify a Current Social Challenge**
  - *Situation:*_____
  - *People involved:*_____
  - *Current difficulty:*_____

- **2. Design Solution Strategy**
  - *List possible approaches:*
    - 1._____
    - 2._____
    - 3._____

- *Choose best approach:*_____
- *Why this might work:*_____

- **3. Implementation Plan**
  - *When I'll try it:*_____
  - *What I'll say/do:*_____
  - *Backup plan if needed:*_____

Weekend: *Integration and Reflection*

Saturday Review:
- *Biggest Success this week:*_____

- Most challenging moment:

_____

- Best new skill learned:

_____

Sunday Planning:

- *Next week's focus:*

_____

- *Skills to practice:*
    - 1._____
    - 2._____
    - 3._____

- *Situations to prepare for:*
    - 1._____
    - 2._____
    - 3._____

Weekly Progress Tracker:

Skill	Start of Week	End of Week	Change
Conversation	3	4	+1
Support			
Group Nav			
Relationship			
Problem Solving			

Step 5: Create Your Social Success Journal

*Let's create your personal journal to track
your social growth and celebrate your wins!*

A. Daily Success Tracker

Date:____/____/____

Skills I Used Today:

☐ *Communication (Example: Active listening during lunch)*

☐ *Reading People (Example: Noticed friend seemed down)*

☐ *Relationship Building (Example: Made plans with new friend)*

☐ *Conflict Resolution (Example: Helped solve group disagreement)*

☐ *Other:*_____

Today's Social Wins:

- *Best moment:*_____
- *What made it work:*_____

- *Thing I'm proud of:*_____
- *Why it matters:*_____

- *New skill I tried:*_____
- *How it went:*_____

Today's Challenges:

- *1. What happened:*_____
  - *How I handled it:*_____
  - *What I learned:*_____

- *2. What happened:*_____
  - *How I handled it:*_____
  - *What I learned:*_____

Tomorrow I Want To:
- *Try this:*_____
- *Practice this:*_____
- *Remember this:*_____

B. Weekly Review

Week Starting: ___ / ___ / ___

This Week's Mood Pattern:
- **Monday:** ☐ Great ☐ Good ☐ Okay ☐ Hard
  - **Why:** _____
    <u>Example:</u> Great - Made new friend in math class!

- **Tuesday:** ☐ Great ☐ Good ☐ Okay ☐ Hard
  - **Why:** _____

- **Wednesday:** ☐ Great ☐ Good ☐ Okay ☐ Hard
  - **Why:** _____

- **Thursday:** ☐ Great ☐ Good ☐ Okay ☐ Hard
  - **Why:** _____

- **Friday:** ☐ Great ☐ Good ☐ Okay ☐ Hard
  - **Why:** _____

- **Weekend:** ☐ Great ☐ Good ☐ Okay ☐ Hard
  - **Why:** _____

Most Important Social Moments:

- *Best interaction:*_____
- *Why it worked:*_____

- *Biggest challenge:*_____
- *How I handled it:*_____
- *New skill I practiced:*_____
- *Progress made:*_____

C. Monthly Progress Check

- *Key Skills Progress:*_____
  (Rate 1-5 and write example for each)

- *Starting Conversations:*
  - *Current level:* ☐ 1 ☐ 2 ☐ 3 ☐ 4 ☐ 5
  - *Example of progress:*_____

- *Active Listening:*
  - *Current level:* ☐ 1 ☐ 2 ☐ 3 ☐ 4 ☐ 5
  - *Example of progress:*_____

- *Reading Body Language:*
  - *Current level:* ☐ 1 ☐ 2 ☐ 3 ☐ 4 ☐ 5
  - *Example of progress:*_____

- *Group Navigation:*
  - *Current level:* ☐ 1 ☐ 2 ☐ 3 ☐ 4 ☐ 5
  - *Example of progress:*_____

D. Monthly Reflection

Looking Back at This Month:

- **New Skills Mastered:**
  - ○ *1. Skill:*_____
    - ▪ *How I use it:*_____
    - ▪ *When it helps most:*_____

  - ○ *2. Skill:*_____
    - ▪ *How I use it:*_____
    - ▪ *When it helps most:*_____

Stronger Relationships:

- *Who:*_____
- *How it improved:*_____
- *What helped:*_____

Challenges Overcome:

- *What was hard:*_____
- *How I managed:*_____
- *What I learned:*_____

Proudest Moments:

- *1.*_____
- *Why it matters:*_____

  _____

- *2.*_____
- *Why it matters:*_____

  _____

Growth Areas:

- *Still working on:*_____
- *Next steps:*_____

E. Support Network Updates

My Social Support Team:

- *Trusted Friends:*
  - *Name:*_____
  - *Best at helping with:*_____
  - *How to reach:*_____

- *Supportive Adults:*
  - *Name:*_____
  - *Best at helping with:*_____
  - *How to reach:*_____

- *New Connections:*
  - *Name:*_____
  - *Best at helping with:*_____
  - *How to reach:*_____

Pro Tips for Your Journal:

- *Write in it right after social interactions while memories are fresh*
- *Be specific about what worked and why*
- *Include both victories and challenges*
- *Look for patterns in what helps you succeed*
- *Celebrate small wins along with big ones*

Chapter 4 Reflection

Take a moment to reflect on your growth in this chapter:

The most valuable skill I learned was:

_____

_____

_____

I'm most proud of trying:

_____

_____

_____

A challenge I overcame was:

_____

_____

_____

Something that surprised me was:

_____

_____

_____

My relationships have changed by:

_____

_____

_____

Looking Forward

Skills I want to keep practicing:

1. _____

2. _____

3. _____

Social situations I feel more confident about:

1. _____

2. _____

3. _____

New goals I want to work toward:

1. _____

2. _____

3. _____

People who can help me continue growing:

1. _____

2. _____

3. _____

Celebrating Your Progress

Check the areas where you've seen improvement:

- ☐ *Starting conversations more easily*
- ☐ *Understanding others better*
- ☐ *Handling conflicts more effectively*
- ☐ *Building stronger relationships*
- ☐ *Supporting others emotionally*

- ☐ Navigating group situations
- ☐ Reading social cues
- ☐ Expressing yourself clearly
- ☐ Setting healthy boundaries
- ☐ Showing empathy to others

Rate your overall progress in social intelligence:
- Beginning of chapter: ☐ 1 ☐ 2 ☐ 3 ☐ 4 ☐ 5
- End of chapter: ☐ 1 ☐ 2 ☐ 3 ☐ 4 ☐ 5

My biggest transformation was:

1. _____

2. _____

3. _____

Congratulations

Remember: *Social intelligence is like a muscle - it gets stronger with practice. Keep using these skills in your daily life, and they'll become more natural over time!*

Social Intelligence Master   Date Completed: ___/___/___

*Now that you've completed your social intelligence training, let's move on to integrating all your new skills into your daily life in **Chapter 5!***

Chapter 5

"Life is like riding a bicycle.
To keep your balance, you
must keep moving."
- Albert Einstein

Lifestyle Integration

Understanding Lifestyle Integration

Think of lifestyle integration like being the director of your own reality show -
you're making sure all the different parts of your life work together smoothly
instead of creating drama!

Real-Life Application:

Taylor used to feel overwhelmed trying to balance school, sports, friends, and sleep. Everything felt disconnected and chaotic. After learning lifestyle integration, they created routines that helped each part of life support the others. Morning exercise helped them focus better in school, better sleep habits improved their sports performance, and planned social time made studying more effective. Instead of feeling pulled apart, their life started fitting together like puzzle pieces!

Sleep Science Lab

Purpose:

To understand and improve your sleep patterns for better emotional and mental functioning.

Materials Needed:

- Pen or pencil
- Your sleep observations
- Willingness to experiment with routines

Real-Life Application

Jordan couldn't figure out why some days were great and others were terrible - until they tracked their sleep. They discovered that scrolling on their phone before bed led to poor sleep, which affected their mood and focus the next day. By creating a better bedtime routine, their whole day improved!

Step 1: Sleep Detective Work

Complete this diary for one week:

Today's Date:_____/_____/_____

Last Night's Sleep:

- *Bedtime:_____*
- *Time I actually fell asleep:_____*
  *(**Example:** Went to bed at 10:00, fell asleep at 10:30)*

- *Number of times I woke up:_____*
- *What woke me:_____*
  *(**Example:** Twice - phone notification, bathroom)*

- *Wake up time:_____*
- *How I woke up:_____*
  *(**Example:** 7:00 AM - alarm clock)*

Total hours of sleep:_____

Rate Your Sleep Quality:
- ☐ *Great - Woke up refreshed*
- ☐ *Good - Mostly rested*
- ☐ *Okay - A bit tired*
- ☐ *Poor - Very tired*

Before-Bed Activities:

- *Check all that you did in the hour before sleep:*
    - ☐ *Used phone/tablet/computer*
    - ☐ *Watched TV*
    - ☐ *Did homework*
    - ☐ *Read a book*
    - ☐ *Took a shower/bath*
    - ☐ *Listened to music*
    - ☐ *Ate or drank something*
    - ☐ *Other:*_____

Today's Results:

- *Morning mood:*
- *Energy level:*
- *Focus ability:*
- *Physical feeling:*

Step 2: Create Your Ideal Sleep Environment

- **Rate your current sleep space (1-5):**
    - *Darkness level:* ☐ *1* ☐ *2* ☐ *3* ☐ *4* ☐ *5*
    - *Quietness:* ☐ *1* ☐ *2* ☐ *3* ☐ *4* ☐ *5*
    - *Temperature:* ☐ *1* ☐ *2* ☐ *3* ☐ *4* ☐ *5*
    - *Comfort:* ☐ *1* ☐ *2* ☐ *3* ☐ *4* ☐ *5*

Sleep Space Improvement Plan:

- *What's working well:*
    - 1._____

- o 2._____
- o 3._____

- What needs to change:
  - o 1. Problem:_____
  - o Solution:_____
  - o When I'll fix it:_____

  - o 2. Problem:_____
  - o Solution:_____
  - o When I'll fix it:_____

  - o 3. Problem:_____
  - o Solution:_____
  - o When I'll fix it:_____

Step 3: Design Your Perfect Bedtime Routine

- *60 Minutes Before Bed:*
- *I will:*_____
  (Example: Put phone on "Do Not Disturb")

- *45 Minutes Before Bed:*
- *I will:*_____
  (Example: Take shower or bath)

- *30 Minutes Before Bed:*
- *I will:*_____
  (Example: Read book or journal)

- 15 Minutes Before Bed:
- I will:_____

   (Example: Deep breathing or stretching)

Step 4: Create Your Wake-Up Success Sequence

My ideal wake-up time:_____

Rate your current morning habits:
- *Easy to wake up:* ☐ 1 ☐ 2 ☐ 3 ☐ 4 ☐ 5
- *Feel refreshed:* ☐ 1 ☐ 2 ☐ 3 ☐ 4 ☐ 5
- *Start day positively:* ☐ 1 ☐ 2 ☐ 3 ☐ 4 ☐ 5

Design your morning sequence:

- *First 5 Minutes:*
- I will:_____

   (Example: Stretch in bed and take deep breaths)

- *Next 10 Minutes:*
- I will:_____

   (Example: Drink water and open curtains)

- *Next 15 Minutes:*
- I will:_____

   (Example: Quick exercise or morning walk)

Step 5: Handle Sleep Challenges

Common Sleep Problems and Solutions:

- *Can't Fall Asleep:*
  - *My usual response:_____*
  - *New strategy to try:_____*

    ([Example:]{.underline} Used to check phone, will try reading instead)

- *Wake Up at Night:*
  - *My usual response:_____*
  - *New strategy to try:_____*

    ([Example:]{.underline} Used to watch clock, will try deep breathing)

- *Feel Tired Next Day:_____*
  - *My usual response:_____*
  - *New strategy to try:_____*

    ([Example:]{.underline} Used to drink lots of coffee, will try morning walk)

- *Create Your Sleep Emergency Kit:*
  - *When I really can't sleep, I will:*
    - *1._____*
    - *2._____*
    - *3._____*

      ([Example:]{.underline} 1. Do calm breathing, 2. Listen to soft music, 3. Write in journal)

Step 6: Weekly Sleep Experiment

Choose one sleep habit to change this week:

- ☐ *Earlier bedtime*
- ☐ *No screens before bed*
- ☐ *Regular wake-up time*
- ☐ *Calming bedtime routine*
- ☐ *Other:*_____

- **My goal:**_____

  (Example: Go to bed 30 minutes earlier each night)

Track Your Results:

Day 1:

- *What I did:*_____
- *How it went:*_____
- *Next day feeling:*_____

Day 2:

- *What I did:*_____
- *How it went:*_____
- *Next day feeling:*_____

Day 3:

- *What I did:*_____
- *How it went:*_____
- *Next day feeling:*_____

Day 4:

- *What I did:*_____
- *How it went:*_____
- *Next day feeling:*_____

Day 5:

- *What I did:*_____
- *How it went:*_____
- *Next day feeling:*_____

Day 6:

- *What I did:*_____
- *How it went:*_____
- *Next day feeling:*_____

Day 7:

- *What I did:*_____
- *How it went:*_____
- *Next day feeling:*_____

Step 7: Create Your Ideal Sleep Schedule

School Days:

- *Bedtime preparation starts:*_____
- *Lights out time:*_____
- *Wake up time:*_____
- *Total sleep hours:*_____

Weekend Plan:
- ☐ Keep same schedule
- ☐ Adjust slightly (How?:_____)
- ☐ Special occasion flexibility plan:_____

Pro Tips for Better Sleep:
- *Think of your bedtime routine like a countdown to sleep*
- *Your morning starts the night before*
- *Small changes can make a big difference*
- *Be patient - new sleep habits take time to develop*

Track Your Sleep Success:
- *7 days across*
- *Space to add draw stars*
- *Room to write daily notes*
- *Example first day filled in with star and note: "Followed new routine, felt great!"]*

- *Weekly goals achieved:_____ out of 7 days*
- *Biggest improvement noticed:_____*
- *Next week's sleep goal:_____*

<u>Remember:</u> Good sleep is like a superpower - it helps everything else in your life work better!

Energy Management System

Purpose:

To understand and manage your energy levels like a pro gamer manages their character's power bar.

Materials Needed:

- Pen or pencil
- Your energy observations
- Willingness to try new strategies

Real-Life Application

Mia used to crash every afternoon and feel totally drained by homework time. After learning to track her energy patterns, she realized that skipping breakfast and spending lunch on social media were draining her energy. By adding protein to breakfast and taking an actual break at lunch, she maintained better energy all day!

Step 1: Energy Mapping

Rate your typical energy level (1-5) during different times of day:

Early Morning (6-8 AM):

- Energy level: ☐ 1 ☐ 2 ☐ 3 ☐ 4 ☐ 5
- I usually feel: _____
- Because I: _____

  (Example: Feel groggy, because I rush to get ready)

Mid-Morning (9-11 AM):

- Energy level: ☐ 1 ☐ 2 ☐ 3 ☐ 4 ☐ 5
- I usually feel: _____
- Because I: _____

  (Example: Alert, because I've had breakfast and started moving)

Lunch Time (12-1 PM):

- Energy level: ☐ 1 ☐ 2 ☐ 3 ☐ 4 ☐ 5
- I usually feel: _____
- Because I: _____

Early Afternoon (2-4 PM):

- Energy level: ☐ 1 ☐ 2 ☐ 3 ☐ 4 ☐ 5
- I usually feel: _____
- Because I: _____

Late Afternoon (4-6 PM):

- Energy level: ☐ 1 ☐ 2 ☐ 3 ☐ 4 ☐ 5
- I usually feel: _____
- Because I: _____

Step 2: Energy Boosters and Drainers

List your personal energy impacts:

Things That Boost My Energy:

- 1._____

  (Example: Taking a short walk)

- 2._____

  (Example: Eating protein-rich snacks)

- 3._____

  (Example: Listening to upbeat music)

- 4._____

- 5._____

Things That Drain My Energy:

- 1._____

  (Example: Too much screen time)

- 2._____

  (Example: Skipping meals)

- 3._____

  (Example: Negative social media)

- 4._____

- 5._____

Step 3: Design Your Energy Management Plan

Morning Energy Launch:

- *First 30 minutes after waking:*
  - *I will:*_____
  - *Avoid:*_____
  - *(Example: Will do 5-minute stretch, avoid checking phone)*

Mid-Morning Energy Check:

- *When I start to drop, I will:*

  _____

- *(Example: Take 3 deep breaths and drink water)*

Afternoon Energy Reset:

- *When the slump hits, I will:*

  _____

- *(Example: Stand up and move for 2 minutes)*

Evening Energy Balance:

- *To maintain good energy, I will:*

  _____

- *(Example: Take short breaks between homework sessions)*

Step 4: Create Your Energy Emergency Kit
When energy is really low:

Quick Fixes (2-5 minutes):

- 1._____
- 2._____
- 3._____

Step 4: Create Your Energy Emergency Kit

- *(Examples: Jump in place, fresh air, power pose)*

Medium Boosts (5-15 minutes):
- 1._____
- 2._____
- 3._____

(Examples: Quick walk, stretching routine, dance break)

Full Reset (15-30 minutes):
- 1._____
- 2._____
- 3._____

(Examples: Power nap, exercise, nature time)

Step 5: Weekly Energy Experiments

Choose one energy habit to try this week:
- ☐ *Morning movement routine*
- ☐ *Regular energy snacks*
- ☐ *Scheduled refresh breaks*
- ☐ *Screen-free times*
- ☐ *Other:_____*

Track Your Results:
- **Monday:**
  - *New habit tried:_____*
  - *Energy level (1-5):_____*
  - *What I noticed:_____*

- **Tuesday:**
  - *New habit tried:*_____
  - *Energy level (1-5):*_____
  - *What I noticed:*_____

- **Wednesday:**
  - *New habit tried:*_____
  - *Energy level (1-5):*_____
  - *What I noticed:*_____

- **Thursday:**
  - *New habit tried:*_____
  - *Energy level (1-5):*_____
  - *What I noticed:*_____

- **Friday:**
  - *New habit tried:*_____
  - *Energy level (1-5):*_____
  - *What I noticed:*_____

- **Saturday:**
  - *New habit tried:*_____
  - *Energy level (1-5):*_____
  - *What I noticed:*_____

- **Sunday:**
  - *New habit tried:*_____
  - *Energy level (1-5):*_____
  - *What I noticed:*_____

Step 5: Create Your Personalized Energy Schedule

Example:

- **6:00-8:00 AM:** Morning Launch
- **Activities:** Quick stretch, healthy breakfast
- **Energy Plan:** Start slow, build momentum

- **8:00-10:00 AM:** Peak Performance
- **Activities:** Important tasks, challenging work
- **Energy Plan:** Use high energy for priority work

- **10:00AM-12:00 PM:** Steady Progress
- **Activities:** _____
- **Energy Plan:** _____

- **12:00-1:00 PM:** Midday Recharge
- **Activities:** _____
- **Energy Plan:** _____

- **5:00-7:00 PM:** Wind Down & Recharge
- **Activities:** _____
- **Energy Plan:** _____

- **7:00-9:00 PM:** Personal Time & Relaxation
- **Activities:** _____
- **Energy Plan:** _____

- **1:00-3:00 PM:** Afternoon Focus
- **Activities:** _____
- **Energy Plan:** _____

- **3:00-5:00 PM:** Power Through
- **Activities:** _____
- **Energy Plan:** _____

- **9:00-10:30 PM:** Evening Reset
- **Activities:** _____
- **Energy Plan:** _____

Pro Tips:

- Think of energy like a rechargeable battery
- Small boosts throughout the day work better than one big fix
- Match activities to your natural energy patterns
- Prevention works better than recovery

Nutrition-Mood Connection

Purpose:

To understand how food affects your mood and energy, like learning which fuel works best for your personal engine.

Materials Needed:

- Pen or pencil
- Food and mood observations
- Willingness to experiment with eating patterns

Real-Life Application

Alex used to get super irritable and couldn't focus by third period. After tracking their food and mood, they realized skipping breakfast was the problem. Adding a morning protein shake and keeping healthy snacks in their backpack helped them stay focused and positive all morning!

Step 1: Food-Mood Detective Work

Today's Date: _____ / _____ / _____

Morning Check-In:
- *Time woke up:*_____
- *First meal/drink:*_____
- *Current mood:*_____
- *Energy level:* ☐ 1 ☐ 2 ☐ 3 ☐ 4 ☐ 5
- *(Example: Woke 7 AM, had coffee only, mood grumpy, energy 2)*

Mid-Morning Update:
- *What I've eaten/drunk:*_____
- *Current mood:*_____
- *Energy level:* ☐ 1 ☐ 2 ☐ 3 ☐ 4 ☐ 5
- *(Example: Had granola bar, mood improving, energy 3)*

Lunch Check:
- *What I ate/drank:*_____
- *Current mood:*_____
- *Energy level:* ☐ 1 ☐ 2 ☐ 3 ☐ 4 ☐ 5
- *Focus level:* ☐ 1 ☐ 2 ☐ 3 ☐ 4 ☐ 5
- *(Example: Sandwich and apple, mood good, energy 4, focus 4)*

Afternoon Update:
- *Snacks/drinks:*_____
- *Current mood:*_____

- Energy level: ☐ 1 ☐ 2 ☐ 3 ☐ 4 ☐ 5
- *(Example: Chips and soda, mood dropping, energy 2)*

Evening Check:
- *Dinner details:*
- *Final mood:*
- *Energy level:* ☐ 1 ☐ 2 ☐ 3 ☐ 4 ☐ 5
- *(Example: Pasta with family, mood relaxed, energy 3)*

Step 2: Create Your Feel-Good Food List

Foods that help me feel great:
- *1._____*
- *When I eat it:_____*
- *How it helps:_____*
- *(Example: Greek yogurt with berries, breakfast, steady energy)*

- *2._____*
- *When I eat it:_____*
- *How it helps:_____*
- *(Example: Turkey sandwich, lunch, good focus)*

- *3._____*
- *When I eat it:_____*
- *How it helps:_____*
- *(Example: Apple with peanut butter, snack, mood boost)*

Foods that don't work well for me:

- 1._____
- When I eat it:_____
- How I feel after:_____
- (Example: Sugary cereal, breakfast, energy crash)

- 2._____
- When I eat it:_____
- How I feel after:_____
- (Example: Just chips for lunch, hungry and cranky)

Step 3: Design Your Personal Power Menu

Breakfast Power Options:

- ☐ Quick choice:_____
- (Example: Banana and peanut butter toast)
- ☐ Sit-down choice:_____
- (Example: Scrambled eggs with cheese and fruit)
- ☐ On-the-go choice:_____
- (Example: Yogurt parfait in to-go cup)

Lunch Power Options:

- ☐ School lunch upgrade:_____
- (Example: Add protein to cafeteria lunch)
- ☐ Packed lunch:_____
- (Example: Wrap, veggies, hummus)
- ☐ Weekend lunch:_____
- (Example: Grain bowl with leftovers)

Smart Snack Options:

- ☐ Backpack-friendly:_____
- (Example: Trail mix in container)
- ☐ Home snacks:_____
- (Example: Apple and cheese)
- ☐ Pre-activity fuel:_____
- (Example: Half sandwich before practice)

▎▷ Step 4: Create Your Mood-Boost Emergency Kit

When I'm Stressed:

- Best foods to eat:_____
- Foods to avoid:_____
- (Example: Eat - Oranges for vitamin C, Avoid - Coffee)

When I'm Tired:

- Best foods to eat:_____
- Foods to avoid:_____
- (Example: Eat - Banana with nuts, Avoid - Sugary drinks)

When I'm Grumpy:

- Best foods to eat:_____
- Foods to avoid:_____
- (Example: Eat - Dark chocolate square, Avoid - Skipping meals)

Step 5: Week-Long Food-Mood Experiment

Choose one eating habit to change:

- ☐ *Add breakfast*
- ☐ *Pack smart snacks*
- ☐ *Drink more water*
- ☐ *Other:* _____

My goal this week: _____

(Example: Eat protein at breakfast every day)

Track your experiment:

Day 1:

- *What I did:* _____
- *How I felt:* _____
- *What I learned:* _____
- *(Example: Had egg on toast, felt more alert in math, learned breakfast helps focus)*

Day 2:

- *What I did:* _____
- *How I felt:* _____
- *What I learned:* _____

Day 3:

- *What I did:* _____
- *How I felt:* _____
- *What I learned:* _____

Day 4:

- *What I did:*_____
- *How I felt:*_____
- *What I learned:*_____

Day 5:

- *What I did:*_____
- *How I felt:*_____
- *What I learned:*_____

Day 6:

- *What I did:*_____
- *How I felt:*_____
- *What I learned:*_____

Day 7:

- *What I did:*_____
- *How I felt:*_____
- *What I learned:*_____

Pro Tips:
- *Small changes can make a big difference*
- *Everyone's body responds differently to foods*
- *Timing of meals matters as much as what you eat*
- *Hydration affects mood too*
- *It's about finding what works for YOU*

Remember: Food is information for your body and brain. The better the information, the better you'll feel and function!

Movement Medicine

Purpose:

To discover how different types of movement can improve your mood, energy, and focus - like having a natural pharmacy of feel-good activities.

Materials Needed:

- Pen or pencil
- Movement tracking
- Willingness to try different activities

Real-Life Application

Jamie felt stuck and anxious studying for exams until they learned about movement medicine. They discovered that a 5-minute dance break helped with stress, a walk around the block cleared their mind, and stretching helped them focus. Now they use different movements like selecting the perfect tool for each situation!

Step 1: Your Movement Inventory

Current Movement Patterns:

Regular Activities:
- ☐ School sports:_____
- ☐ Dance/martial arts:_____
- ☐ Walking/biking:_____
- ☐ Other:_____

Rate how you feel during these activities:
- Energy: ☐ 1 ☐ 2 ☐ 3 ☐ 4 ☐ 5
- Mood: ☐ 1 ☐ 2 ☐ 3 ☐ 4 ☐ 5
- Focus after: ☐ 1 ☐ 2 ☐ 3 ☐ 4 ☐ 5

Movement Wishes:
- Activities I'd like to try:_____
- What stops me:_____
- How I could start:_____

Step 2: Create Your Movement Medicine Cabinet

Quick Energy Boost (2-5 minutes):
- ☐ Jumping jacks:_____sets of_____
- ☐ Dancing to one song
- ☐ Walking up and down stairs
- ☐ Other:_____

  (_Example:_ 20 jumping jacks when tired in class)

Stress Relief (5-15 minutes):
- ☐ *Walking outside*
- ☐ *Stretching routine*
- ☐ *Punching air/shadow boxing*
- ☐ *Other:_____*

  (Example: 10-minute walk after difficult test)

Focus Enhancement (5-10 minutes):
- ☐ *Yoga poses*
- ☐ *Balance exercises*
- ☐ *Slow stretching*
- ☐ *Other:_____*

  (Example: 5 minutes of stretching before homework)

Mood Lift (10-20 minutes):
- ☐ *Dance party*
- ☐ *Sports practice*
- ☐ *Bike ride*
- ☐ *Other:_____*

  (Example: Dancing to favorite playlist when feeling down)

Step 3: Design Your Daily Movement Menu

Morning Energizer:
- *Time:_____*
- *Activity:_____*
- *Duration:_____*
- *(Example: 7:30 AM, 5-minute stretching routine)*

Mid-Morning Break:
- *Time:*_____
- *Activity:*_____
- *Duration:*_____
- *(Example: 10:30 AM, quick hallway walk between classes)*

Lunch Movement:
- *Time:*_____
- *Activity:*_____
- *Duration:*_____
- *(Example: 12:15 PM, walking with friends after eating)*

Afternoon Reset:
- *Time:*_____
- *Activity:*_____
- *Duration:*_____
- *(Example: 3:30 PM, 15-minute bike ride after school)*

Evening Activity:
- *Time:*_____
- *Activity:*_____
- *Duration:*_____
- *(Example: 7:00 PM, dancing while doing chores)*

Step 4: Movement Experiments

Try these mini-challenges and note how they affect you:

Morning Movement:
- *What I tried:*_____

- *How I felt before:*_____
- *How I felt after:*_____
- *(Example: 10 stretches before breakfast, felt stiff, then energized)*

Study Break Motion:
- *What I tried:*_____
- *How I felt before:*_____
- *How I felt after:*_____
- *(Example: Jump rope for 2 minutes, felt stuck, then clearer thinking)*

Stress-Relief Movement:
- *What I tried:*_____
- *How I felt before:*_____
- *How I felt after:*_____
- *(Example: Wall pushups when anxious, felt tense, then calmer)*

Step 5: Create Your Movement Success Strategies

- *When I "don't feel like it":*
- *I can:*_____
- *(Example: Just commit to 2 minutes, then decide)*

- *When I'm "too tired":*
- *I can:*_____
- *(Example: Gentle walking instead of intense exercise)*

- *When I'm "not motivated":*
- *I can:*_____
- *(Example: Ask a friend to join me)*

Step 6: Build Your Movement Support System

Movement Buddies:
- ☐ *Friends who'll join me:*
- ☐ *Family who'll support me:*
- ☐ *Online resources:*
- ☐ *Other helpers:*_____

Track Your Movement Medicine Results:

Example:
Monday 3:30 PM
- *Type of movement: 10-minute dance break*
- *How I felt before: Stressed about math homework, tired from sitting*
- *How I felt after: More energized, clearer head, ready to try math again*
- *What I learned: Short dance breaks help me reset when stuck on homework*

Tuesday
- *Type of movement:*_____
- *How I felt before:*_____
- *How I felt after:*_____
- *What I learned:*_____

Wednesday
- *Type of movement:*_____
- *How I felt before:*_____
- *How I felt after:*_____
- *What I learned:*_____

Thursday

- *Type of movement:*_____
- *How I felt before:*_____
- *How I felt after:*_____
- *What I learned:*_____

Friday

- *Type of movement:*_____
- *How I felt before:*_____
- *How I felt after:*_____
- *What I learned:*_____

Saturday

- *Type of movement:*_____
- *How I felt before:*_____
- *How I felt after:*_____
- *What I learned:*_____

Sunday

- *Type of movement:*_____
- *How I felt before:*_____
- *How I felt after:*_____
- *What I learned:*_____

Pro Tips:

- Any movement counts
- Start small and build gradually
- Match the movement to your mood and energy
- Find what feels good to YOU
- Remember: movement is medicine, not punishment

Remember: Movement is like having a pharmacy in your body - there's a type of movement medicine for every situation!

Time Management Mastery

Purpose:

To learn how to manage your time like a skilled video game player manages their resources - strategically and effectively.

Materials Needed:

- Pen or pencil
- Time tracking
- Openness to new routines

Real-Life Application

Luis felt constantly overwhelmed with homework, soccer practice, and family responsibilities. After learning time management, they started "time blocking" their day and setting specific study times. The result? Less stress, better grades, and even more free time to spend with friends!

Step 1: Time Detective Work

Track where your time actually goes:

Morning Routine:
- *What I do:*_____
- *How long it takes:*_____
- *Time wasters:*_____
- *Time savers:*_____
  (Example: Spend 15 minutes looking for clothes, could pick them night before)

School Day:
- *Free periods:*_____
- *Study times:*_____
- *Social time:*_____
- *Wasted time:*_____
  (Example: Spend 30 minutes scrolling between classes)

After School:
- *Activities:*_____
- *Homework time:*_____
- *Family time:*_____
- *Free time:*_____
  (Example: 2 hours practice, 1 hour social media, 2 hours homework)

Evening:
- *Regular activities:*_____
- *Preparation for tomorrow:*_____
- *Relaxation time:*_____
- *Bedtime routine:*_____
  (Example: 1 hour TV, no prep for tomorrow, rushed morning)

Step 2: Create Your Ideal Schedule Blueprint

Morning Power Hour:
- *Must do:*_____
- *Could eliminate:*_____
- *Could combine:*_____
  (Example: Must eat breakfast, eliminate phone checking, combine getting ready with review notes)

School Success Windows:
- Best focus times:_____
- Study spots:_____
- Break times:_____
  (Example: Best focus 10-11 AM, library during free period)

After School Power Blocks:
- *First priority:*_____
- *Second priority:*_____
- *Energy level:* ☐ 1 ☐ 2 ☐ 3 ☐ 4 ☐ 5
- *Best order of tasks:*_____
  (Example: Homework first while energy high, then practice)

Evening Optimization:
- *Most important:*_____
- *Preparation tasks:*_____
- *Relaxation needs:*_____
  (Example: 30 minutes prep for tomorrow, then relax)

Step 3: Design Your Focus Zones

Study Zone:
- *Location:*_____
- *What I need:*_____
- *Distractions to remove:*_____
- *Focus helpers:*_____

  (Example: Desk in room, need good light, remove phone, use timer)

Activity Zone:
- *Location:*_____
- *What I need:*_____
- *Time slot:*_____
- *Energy management:*_____

  (Example: Sports field, need equipment ready, 3-5 PM, healthy snack before)

Social Zone:
- *Time blocks:*_____
- *Boundaries:*_____
- *Balance plan:*_____

  (Example: Lunch and after homework, set time limits, balance in-person and online)

Rest Zone:
- *When needed:*_____
- *How long:*_____
- *Reset activities:*_____

  (Example: After big tests, 30 minutes, quiet music and stretching)

Step 4: Create Your Time Management Tools

Priority Sorter:

Must Do Today:
- 1._____
- 2._____
- 3._____

Should Do Soon:
- 1._____
- 2._____
- 3._____

Could Do Later:
- 1._____
- 2._____
- 3._____

Time Blocking Template:

Early Morning Block:
- *Time:*_____
- *Activities:*_____
- *Energy Level:*_____

Mid-Day Block:
- *Time:*_____
- *Activities:*_____
- *Energy Level:*_____

Afternoon Block:
- *Time:*_____

- Activities:_____
- Energy Level:_____

Evening Block:
- Time:_____
- Activities:_____
- Energy Level:_____

Step 5: Develop Your Time Rescue Plans

When Running Late:
- Quick fixes: _____
- Priority shifts:_____
- Communication plan:_____

    (Example: Quick fixes - combine tasks, Priority - identify most important, Communication - text ahead)

When Overwhelmed:
- First response:_____
- Break it down:_____
- Ask for help:_____

    (Example: Take three breaths, list small steps, ask teacher for guidance)

When Distracted:
- Notice triggers: _____
- Reset actions: _____
- Get back on track:_____

    (Example: Notice phone notifications, put phone away, use 5-minute focus timer)

Pro Tips:

- *Time management is a skill you can learn*
- *Small changes add up to big results*
- *What works for others might not work for you*
- *Keep adjusting until you find your perfect system*
- *Balance is more important than perfection*

Remember: *Good time management isn't about doing more - it's about doing what matters most to you!*

Environment Design

Purpose:

To create spaces that support your goals and well-being, like designing different game levels for different purposes.

Materials Needed:

- Pen or pencil
- Space assessment
- Creative thinking
- Willingness to reorganize

Real-Life Application

Sofia couldn't focus on homework in her room because everything reminded her of distractions - phone on the desk, TV visible from her chair, social media notifications popping up on her laptop. After redesigning her study space, with a dedicated homework spot facing away from distractions and her phone in a special "parking spot," her focus and grades improved dramatically!

Step 1: Space Mapping

- Space: Bedroom desk area
- Current use: Homework, gaming, social media, eating snacks
- How it makes me feel: Scattered, distracted, unproductive
- Ideal use: Focused study space, creative projects
- Changes needed: Clear desk of non-study items, face desk away from TV, create separate snack area

Include the 3 areas below with these same categories:
- Space
- Current use
- How it makes me feel
- Ideal use
- Changes needed]

Map Your Key Spaces:

Study Space:
- Location:_____
- Current setup:_____
- Focus level there: ☐ 1 ☐ 2 ☐ 3 ☐ 4 ☐ 5
- Distractions present:_____
- Improvements needed:_____

Sleep Space:
- Location:_____
- Current setup:_____
- Sleep quality there: ☐ 1 ☐ 2 ☐ 3 ☐ 4 ☐ 5
- Distractions present:_____
- Improvements needed:_____

Activity Space:

- *Location:*_____
- *Current setup:*_____
- *Energy level there:* ☐ 1 ☐ 2 ☐ 3 ☐ 4 ☐ 5
- *Limitations present:*_____
- *Improvements needed:*_____

Step 2: Design Your Focus Zones

- *Zone: Study Focus Zone*
- *Location: Corner of bedroom*
- *Essential items: Desk, good lamp, comfortable chair*
- *Remove: Phone, gaming equipment, snacks*
- *Add: Timer, study supplies, water bottle*
- *Mood elements: Plant, inspiring quote, calm colors*
- *When to use: 4-6 PM homework time*
- *Rules: No phone zone, clean desk before starting*

Create Your Zone Rules:

Study Zone Rules:

- *Time used:*_____
- *Items allowed:*_____
- *Items banned:*_____
- *Sound level:*_____
- *Break schedule:*_____

Sleep Zone Rules:_____

- *Start wind-down:*_____
- *Items allowed:*_____

- *Items banned:*_____
- *Atmosphere needs:*_____
- *Morning setup:*_____

Activity Zone Rules:
- *Times available:*_____
- *Equipment needed:*_____
- *Safety checks:*_____
- *Clean-up routine:*_____
- *Sharing guidelines:*_____

Step 3: Create Your Environment Success Tools

Tool: Study Session Setup Checklist
- ☐ *Clear desk surface*
- ☐ *Gather all materials needed*
- ☐ *Fill water bottle*
- ☐ *Set phone in "parking spot"*
- ☐ *Turn on good lighting*
- ☐ *Set timer for 25 minutes*
- ☐ *Put on focus music playlist*
- *Status: Ready to focus!*

Design Your Support Systems:

Focus Support:
- ☐ *Good lighting*
- ☐ *Comfortable seating*
- ☐ *Supply station*
- ☐ *Timer system*

- Other:_____

Sleep Support:
- ☐ Dark curtains
- ☐ White noise
- ☐ Temperature control
- ☐ Comfort items
- ☐ Other:_____

Energy Support:
- ☐ Movement space
- ☐ Fresh air access
- ☐ Hydration station
- ☐ Snack spot
- ☐ Other:_____

Step 4: Environment Experiments

- **Experiment:** Moving desk to face wall instead of window
- **Day 1:** Less distracted by outside movement
- **Day 2:** Stayed focused longer on homework
- **Day 3:** Found myself getting up less during study time
- **Result:** Keep this change - helps focus!

Try these changes:

Study Space Experiment:
- Change tried:_____
- Days tracked:_____
- Results noticed:_____
- Keep or adjust?:_____

Sleep Space Experiment:

- *Change tried:*_____
- *Days tracked:*_____
- *Results noticed:*_____
- *Keep or adjust?:*_____

Energy Space Experiment:

- *Change tried:*_____
- *Days tracked:*_____
- *Results noticed:*_____
- *Keep or adjust?:*_____

Pro Tips:

- *Small changes can make a big difference*
- *Test one change at a time*
- *Give each change at least three days*
- *Adjust based on what works for YOU*
- *Environment shapes behavior*

Remember: *Your space should work for you, not against you!*

Chapter 5 Reflection

Take a moment to reflect on your progress:

The most helpful change I've made is:

I've noticed these positive effects:

- 1._____
- 2._____
- 3._____

My biggest challenge was:

_____
_____
_____

How I handled it:_____

Something that surprised me was:

_____
_____
_____

My daily life has improved by:

_____
_____
_____

Looking Forward

Habits I want to strengthen:

- 1._____
- 2._____
- 3._____

New routines I want to try:

- 1._____
- 2._____
- 3._____

Areas I still want to work on:

- 1._____
- 2._____
- 3._____

People who can support my changes:

- 1._____
- 2._____
- 3._____

Rate Your Progress:

Sleep Quality:

- *Start of chapter:* ☐1 ☐2 ☐3 ☐4 ☐5
- *End of chapter:* ☐1 ☐2 ☐3 ☐4 ☐5
- *Example improvement: Better morning routine helps me wake up easier*

Energy Management:

- *Start of chapter:* ☐1 ☐2 ☐3 ☐4 ☐5
- *End of chapter:* ☐1 ☐2 ☐3 ☐4 ☐5
- *Example improvement: Afternoon walks prevent energy crashes*

Celebrating Your Progress

Check the improvements you've noticed:

- ☐ *Better sleep quality*
- ☐ *More consistent energy*
- ☐ *Improved mood stability*
- ☐ *Better focus*
- ☐ *More physical activity*
- ☐ *Better organized spaces*
- ☐ *More productive time use*
- ☐ *Healthier eating habits*
- ☐ *Better morning routine*
- ☐ *Calmer evening routine*

My biggest lifestyle transformation was:

_____

_____

_____

<u>**Remember:**</u> *Small changes add up to big improvements. Keep building on what works for you!*

Lifestyle Integration Master   Date Completed:___/___/___

*Now that you've learned to integrate healthy habits into your daily life, let's move on to **Chapter 6** where we'll explore future planning!*

Chapter 6

Future Planning

"The best way to
predict your future
is to create it."
- Abraham Lincoln

▌▶ Understanding Future Planning

Think of future planning like being the director of your own life movie - you get
to imagine different possible scenes, choose which ones you want to create, and
figure out how to make them happen!

Real-Life Application:

Kai felt overwhelmed thinking about the future until they learned how to break it down into smaller pieces. Instead of worrying about "the rest of my life," they started with one goal: joining the school newspaper. They mapped out small steps like taking a writing class and submitting practice articles. Each small success built their confidence to plan bigger goals!

Vision Creation Studio

Purpose:

To explore and design possible futures that excite and motivate you, like creating concept art for your life's movie

Materials Needed:

- Pen or pencil
- Imagination
- Openness to possibilities

Step 1: Future Scene Exploration

- **Scene:** *One Year From Now*
- **Location:** *High school newspaper office*
- **What I'm doing:** *Editing my first front-page story*
- **How I feel:** *Proud, confident, excited*
- **Skills I used:** *Writing, interviewing, meeting deadlines*
- **Who's there:** *Other student journalists, mentor teacher*
- **How I got there:** *Took journalism class, practiced writing, submitted articles*

Create Your Future Scenes:

One Year From Now:

- *Where I am:*_____
- *What I'm doing:*_____
- *How I feel:*_____
- *Who's with me:*_____
- *What's different:*_____

Three Years From Now:

- *Where I am:*_____
- *What I'm doing:*_____
- *How I feel:*_____
- *Who's with me:*_____
- *What's different:*_____

Five Years From Now:

- *Where I am:* _____
- *What I'm doing:* _____
- *How I feel:* _____
- *Who's with me:* _____
- *What's different:* _____

Ten Years From Now:

- *Where I am:* _____
- *What I'm doing:* _____
- *How I feel:* _____
- *Who's with me:* _____
- *What's different:* _____

Twenty Years From Now:

- *Where I am:* _____
- *What I'm doing:* _____
- *How I feel:* _____
- *Who's with me:* _____
- *What's different:* _____

Step 2: Explore Your Interest Areas

 Interest:
Writing

 What I love about it:
Creating stories that move people

 **Current skills:**
Good grammar, creative ideas

 Skills to develop:
Interviewing, editing

 Possible paths:
Journalism, creative writing, communications

 **Next step:** *Join school newspaper club*

Map Your Interests:

Interest Area 1:
- *What draws me to this:*_____
- *Current strengths:*_____
- *Room to grow:*_____
- *Possible directions:*_____
- *Next step:*_____

Interest Area 2:
- *What draws me to this:*_____
- *Current strengths:*_____
- *Room to grow:*_____
- *Possible directions:*_____
- *Next step:*_____

Interest Area 3:

- *What draws me to this:*_____
- *Current strengths:*_____
- *Room to grow:*_____
- *Possible directions:*_____
- *Next step:*_____

Step 3: Design Your Future Lifestyle

- **Area:** *Daily Schedule*
- **Current:** *Rush to school, tired all day, homework late at night*
- **Future Vision:** *Early start, productive day, balanced evening*
- **Changes needed:** *Better sleep routine, organized study time*
- **First step:** *Set up morning routine with prep the night before*

Your Lifestyle Design:

Learning Life:

- *Current situation:*_____
- *Future vision:*_____
- *Changes needed:*_____
- *First steps:*_____

Work/Activity Balance:

- *Current situation:*_____
- *Future vision:*_____
- *Changes needed:*_____
- *First steps:*_____

Social Connections:

- *Current situation:*_____
- *Future vision:*_____
- *Changes needed:*_____
- *First steps:*_____

Health and Energy:

- *Current situation:*_____
- *Future vision:*_____
- *Changes needed:*_____
- *First steps:*_____

Creative Expression:

- *Current situation:*_____
- *Future vision:*_____
- *Changes needed:*_____
- *First steps:*_____

Personal Growth:

- *Current situation:*_____
- *Future vision:*_____
- *Changes needed:*_____
- *First steps:*_____

Step 4: Create Your Vision Testing Ground

- **Vision Test:** *Try writing for school newspaper*
- **Mini-experiment:** *Write one practice article*
- **Time frame:** *Two weeks*
- **What worked:** *Found interesting topic, enjoyed interviews*
- **Challenges:** *Meeting deadlines, organizing information*
- **Next step:** *Show draft to English teacher for feedback*

Test Your Future Ideas:

Vision Test 1:
- *What I'll try:*_____
- *Mini-experiment:*_____
- *Time frame:*_____
- *Success looks like:*_____
- *Challenges:*_____
- *Support needed:*_____
- *Next step:*_____

Vision Test 2:
- *What I'll try:*_____
- *Mini-experiment:*_____
- *Time frame:*_____
- *Success looks like:*_____
- *Challenges:*_____
- *Support needed:*_____
- *Next step:*_____

Vision Test 3:

- *What I'll try:*_____
- *Mini-experiment:*_____
- *Time frame:*_____
- *Success looks like:*_____
- *Challenges:*_____
- *Support needed:*_____
- *Next step:*_____

Vision Test 4:

- *What I'll try:*_____
- *Mini-experiment:*_____
- *Time frame:*_____
- *Success looks like:*_____
- *Challenges:*_____
- *Support needed:*_____
- *Next step:*_____

Step 5: Build Your Vision Support Team

- **Role:** *Writing Mentor*
- **Who:** *Ms. Garcia, English teacher*
- **How they can help:** *Review articles, give feedback*
- **How to ask:** *Stay after class, schedule meeting time*
- **What to share:** *Goals, current work, specific questions*

Your Support Network:

Mentor/Guide:
- *Who:*_____
- *Their experience:*_____
- *How they can help:*_____
- *How to connect:*_____

Cheerleader:
- *Who:*_____
- *Their experience:*_____
- *How they can help:*_____
- *How to connect:*_____

Reality Checker:
- *Who:*_____
- *Their experience:*_____
- *How they can help:*_____
- *How to connect:*_____

Skill Builder:
- *Who:*_____
- *Their experience:*_____
- *How they can help:*_____
- *How to connect:*_____

Step 6: Create Your Vision Journey Map

- **Starting Point:** *Interested in writing*
- **First milestone:** *Write for school paper (3 months)*
- **Second milestone:** *Editor position (1 year)*
- **Third milestone:** *Journalism program (2 years)*
- **Dream destination:** *Professional writer*
- **Alternative paths:** *Communications, teaching, publishing*
- **Possible obstacles:** *Time management, confidence*
- **Solutions:** *Create schedule, join writing group*

Map Your Journey:

Starting Point:

- *Where I am now:_____*
- *Current skills:_____*
- *Resources I have:_____*

Milestones:

- *3 months:_____*
- *6 months:_____*
- *1 year:_____*
- *2 years:_____*
- *5 years:_____*

- *Dream destination:_____*

Alternative paths:

- Path 1: _____
- Path 2: _____
- Path 3: _____

Possible Obstacles:

- Challenge 1:_____
- Solution:_____

- Challenge 2:_____
- Solution:_____

- Challenge 3:_____
- Solution:_____

Pro Tips:
- *Your vision can change - that's okay!*
- *Start with what excites you*
- *Break big dreams into small steps*
- *Test ideas before committing*
- *Keep what works, adjust what doesn't*

Remember: *The future is like a story you get to write - make it one you'll enjoy reading!*

Goal Setting Workshop

Purpose:

To transform your visions into achievable goals, like turning a game idea into actual playable levels.

Materials Needed:

- Pen or pencil
- Your vision ideas from Exercise 73
- Strategic thinking skills

Real-Life Application

Maria had a dream of starting a school club for environmental awareness but felt overwhelmed about where to start. Using goal-setting techniques, she broke it down into smaller steps: research other clubs, find a teacher sponsor, create a plan, recruit five core members. Within two months, her club held its first meeting!

Step 1: Goal Discovery Workshop

- **Area:** *Academic Success*
- **Big Dream:** *Graduate with honors*
- **Why it matters:** *Pride in achievement, college options*
- **Current situation:** *B average, struggle with math*
- **90-day goal:** *Raise math grade to B+*
- **Next action:** *Schedule meeting with math teacher*
- **Support needed:** *Tutor, study group*
- **How to track:** *Weekly grade checks*

Explore Your Goals:

Academic Goals:

- *Big dream:* _____
- *Why it matters:* _____
- *Current reality:* _____
- *90-day target:* _____
- *Next Action:* _____
- *Support needed:* _____
- *How to track:* _____

Personal Growth Goals:

- *Big dream:* _____
- *Why it matters:* _____
- *Current reality:* _____
- *90-day target:* _____
- *Next Action:* _____
- *Support needed:* _____
- *How to track:* _____

Social Goals:

- *Big dream:*_____
- *Why it matters:*_____
- *Current reality:*_____
- *90-day target:*_____
- *Next Action:*_____
- *Support needed:*_____
- *How to track:*_____

Step 2: Goal Reality Check

- **Goal:** *Join school basketball team*
- **Specific:** *Make junior varsity team by November tryouts*
- **Measurable:** *Can run full court 10 times, make 7/10 free throws*
- **Achievable:** *Currently can run 5 times, make 4/10 shots*
- **Realistic:** *Have 3 months to practice, access to court*
- **Time-bound:** *Tryouts in 90 days*
- **Action plan:** *Practice 1 hour daily, join summer camp*
- **Progress tracking:** *Weekly skills test, endurance check*

Test Your Goals:

Goal 1:

- *Make it Specific:*_____
- *Make it Measurable:*_____
- *Check if Achievable:*_____
- *Confirm it's Realistic:*_____
- *Set Time Frame:*_____
- *Action Steps:*_____
- *Track Progress:*_____

Goal 2:

- *Make it Specific:*_____
- *Make it Measurable:*_____
- *Check if Achievable:*_____
- *Confirm it's Realistic:*_____
- *Set Time Frame:*_____

Step 3: Create Your Goal Achievement System

Goal: *Improve Spanish grade*

- **Daily actions:**
    - *Review vocabulary 15 minutes*
    - *Listen to Spanish podcast on way to school*
    - *Practice with language app before bed*
- **Weekly checks:**
    - *Quiz scores*
    - *New words learned*
    - *Conversation practice done*
- **Monthly milestone:**
    - *Class presentation*
    - *Vocabulary test*
    - *Speaking assessment*
- **Reward system:**
    - ***Daily:*** *Check mark in tracker*
    - ***Weekly:*** *Extra social media time*
    - ***Monthly:*** *New playlist download*

Design Your System:

Goal System 1:
- **Daily actions:**

1. _____
2. _____
3. _____

- **Weekly checks:**

1. _____
2. _____
3. _____

- **Monthly milestones:**

1. _____
2. _____
3. _____

- **Rewards:**
  - *Daily:*_____
  - *Weekly:*_____
  - *Monthly:*_____

Goal System 2:
- **Daily actions:**

1.
_____
2. _____
3. _____
_____

- **Weekly checks:**

1. _____
2. _____
3. _____

- **Monthly milestones:**

1. _____
2. _____
3. _____

- **Rewards:**
  - *Daily:* _____
  - *Weekly:* _____
  - *Monthly:* _____

Step 4: Build Your Goal Tracker

My Goal Tracker:

- **This Week's Focus:** _____
  (Example: "Learn Spanish basics")

Weekly Progress Daily Check:
- **Monday**
  - ☐ *Morning:* _____ *(like "10 min study")*
  - ☐ *Afternoon:* _____ *(like "practice lunch")*
  - ☐ *Evening:* _____ *(like "review 3 words")*

- **Tuesday**
  - ☐ *Morning:* _____
  - ☐ *Afternoon:* _____
  - ☐ *Evening:* _____

- **Wednesday**
  - ☐ *Morning:* _____

- ☐ *Afternoon:*_____
- ☐ *Evening:*_____

- **Thursday**
  - ☐ *Morning:*_____
  - ☐ *Afternoon:*_____
  - ☐ *Evening:*_____

- **Friday**
  - ☐ *Morning:*_____
  - ☐ *Afternoon:*_____
  - ☐ *Evening:*_____

- **Saturday**
  - ☐ *Morning:*_____
  - ☐ *Afternoon:*_____
  - ☐ *Evening:*_____

- **Sunday**
  - ☐ *Morning:*_____
  - ☐ *Afternoon:*_____
  - ☐ *Evening:*_____

- **Monthly milestones:**
  - ○ *What's Working:*_____
  - ○ *Need to Fix:*_____
  - ○ *Next Week's Plan:*_____

- **Monthly Milestone:**_____
  [Example: "Have a basic conversation by June 30"]

- **Monthly Milestone:**_____

  (Example: "Have a basic conversation by June 30")

Step 5: Create Your Goal Emergency Plans

When Plans Don't Go as Expected:

- **Warning signs:** Things aren't working the way you thought, or unexpected obstacles show up.
- **Quick fixes:** Adjust your approach or simplify the plan for now.
- **Prevention:** Have a backup plan ready before starting.
- **Support needed:** Talk to someone who has faced similar challenges to get advice.

Your Emergency Plans:

- **When Time Gets Tight:**
  - *Warning signs:*_____
  - *Quick fixes:*_____
  - *Prevention:*_____
  - *Support needed:*_____

- **When Motivation Drops:**
  - *Warning signs:*_____
  - *Quick fixes:*_____
  - *Prevention:*_____
  - *Support needed:*_____

- **When Obstacles Appear:**
  - *Warning signs:*_____
  - *Quick fixes:*_____
  - *Prevention:*_____
  - *Support needed:*_____

- **Falling Behind in Class:**
  - *Warning signs:*_____
  - *Quick fixes:*_____
  - *Prevention:*_____
  - *Support needed:*_____

For these next two you pick a situation:

- _____
  - *Warning signs:*_____
  - *Quick fixes:*_____
  - *Prevention:*_____
  - *Support needed:*_____

- _____
  - *Warning signs:*_____
  - *Quick fixes:*_____
  - *Prevention:*_____
  - *Support needed:*_____

Step 6: Design Your Goal Celebration System

Your Celebration System:

Goal: Finish reading one book a month

- **Daily Wins:**
    - *What counts: Read 10 pages a day*
    - *How to celebrate: Play a favorite song*
    - *Who to tell: Share progress with a friend*

- **Weekly Victories:**
    - *What counts: Read three chapters by the end of the week*
    - *How to celebrate: Watch one episode of a favorite TV show*
    - *Who to tell: Update a parent or teacher*

- **Monthly Milestones:**
    - *What counts: Finish the entire book for the month*
    - *How to celebrate: Go out for a milkshake or smoothie*
    - *Who to tell: Share with the book club or post on social media*

Now it is your turn to design your goal celebration system:

Your Celebration System:
- **Daily Wins:**
    - *What counts:_____*
    - *How to celebrate:_____*
    - *Who to tell:_____*

- **Weekly Victories:**
  - *What counts:_____*
  - *How to celebrate:_____*
  - *Who to tell:_____*

- **Monthly Milestones:**
  - *What counts:_____*
  - *How to celebrate:_____*
  - *Who to tell:_____*

Pro Tips:
- *Goals should excite and challenge you*
- *Break big goals into small steps*
- *Track progress consistently*
- *Celebrate all wins, big and small*
- *Adjust plans when needed*
- *Keep your why in mind*
- *Goal Wisdom to Remember:*
- *Goals are about growth, not perfection*
- *Small steps lead to big changes*
- *Setbacks are normal and helpful*
- *Support makes success easier*
- *Consistency beats intensity*
- *Your goals can evolve as you do*

Future Skills Development

Purpose:

To identify and develop the skills you'll need for your future goals, like leveling up your character in a game before taking on bigger challenges.

Materials Needed:

- Pen or pencil
- Your goals from Exercise 74
- Learning mindset

Real-Life Application

David wanted to work in game design but didn't know where to start. By mapping out needed skills, he discovered he could begin with free online coding courses, join the school's computer club, and practice designing simple games. Each small skill he learned brought him closer to his goal!

Step 1: Skills Inventory Check

- **Skill Area:** *Computer Programming*
- **Current level:** *Beginner (1/5)*
- **What I can do now:** *Basic HTML, simple websites*
- **What I need to learn:** *JavaScript, Python*
- **Why it matters:** *Need for game design career*
- **How to improve:** *Online courses, coding club*
- **Next step:** *Sign up for Code Academy course*
- **Timeline:** *Start next week*

Map Your Skills:

Technical Skills:
- *Current level:* ☐ 1 ☐ 2 ☐ 3 ☐ 4 ☐ 5
- *Can do now:* _____
- *Need to learn:* _____
- *Why it matters:* _____
- *How to improve:* _____
- *Next step:* _____

Communication Skills:
- *Current level:* ☐ 1 ☐ 2 ☐ 3 ☐ 4 ☐ 5
- *Can do now:* _____
- *Need to learn:* _____
- *Why it matters:* _____
- *How to improve:* _____
- *Next step:* _____

Creative Skills:

- *Current level:* ☐ 1 ☐ 2 ☐ 3 ☐ 4 ☐ 5
- *Can do now:*_____
- *Need to learn:*_____
- *Why it matters:*_____
- *How to improve:*_____
- *Next step:*_____

Step 2: Design Your Learning Path

- **Skill:** *JavaScript Programming*
- **Starting point:** *Know basic HTML*
- **3-month goal:** *Build simple interactive website*
- **Learning resources:**
  - *Online course: Intro to JavaScript*
  - *Practice: Code 30 minutes daily*
  - *Project: Create personal website*
- **Checkpoints:**
  - *Week 1-4: Complete basics course*
  - *Week 5-8: Practice small projects*
  - *Week 9-12: Build final project*
  - *Support needed: Coding mentor, study group*

Create Your Learning Paths:

- **Path 1:**
  - *Skill focus:*_____
  - *Starting point:*_____
  - *3-month goal:*_____

- Learning resources:_____
- Weekly plan:_____
- Support needed:_____

- **Path 2:**
  - Skill focus: _____
  - Starting point:_____
  - 3-month goal:_____
  - Learning resources:_____
  - Weekly plan:_____
  - Support needed:_____

Step 3: Create Your Practice Plan

- **Skill:** *JavaScript Coding*
- **Daily practice:** *30 minutes coding exercise*
- **Weekly project:** *Create one interactive element*
- **Monthly goal:** *Complete website homepage*
- **Practice tools:**
  - Laptop with coding software
  - Online tutorials
  - Practice exercises
- **Progress measures:**
  - Projects completed
  - New functions learned
  - Debugging success rate

Design Your Practice:

- **Skill Practice 1:**
    - *Daily time:*_____
    - *Weekly project:*_____
    - *Monthly goal:*_____
    - *Tools needed:*_____
    - *How to measure:*_____

- **Skill Practice 2:**
    - *Daily time:*_____
    - *Weekly project:*_____
    - *Monthly goal:*_____
    - *Tools needed:*_____
    - *How to measure:*_____

- **Skill Practice 3:**
    - *Daily time:*_____
    - *Weekly project:*_____
    - *Monthly goal:*_____
    - *Tools needed:*_____
    - *How to measure:*_____

Step 4: Build Your Learning Support System

- **Learning Need:** *JavaScript Help*
- **Online resources:**
  - *Tutorial website*
  - *Coding forum*
  - *Video lessons*
- **People support:**
  - *Computer teacher*
  - *Online mentor*
  - *Study group*
- **Practice partners:**
  - *Coding club members*
  - *Online community*
- **When to ask for help:**
  - *Stuck for 30 minutes*
  - *Need code review*
  - *New concept confusion*

Your Support Systems:

- **Learning Support 1:**
  - *Online resources:*_____
  - *People helpers:*_____
  - *Practice groups:*_____
  - *When to use:*_____

- **Learning Support 2:**
  - *Online resources:*_____
  - *People helpers:*_____
  - *Practice groups:*_____
  - *When to use:*_____

Step 5: Create Your Skill Testing Ground

- **Skill Test:** Basic JavaScript
- **Mini-project:** Create interactive button
- **Time frame:** One week
- **Success markers:**
  - *Button changes color when clicked*
  - *Adds text when hovered*
  - *Works on different browsers*
- **Learning outcome:**
  - *Event handling mastered*
  - *Debug skills improved*
- **Next challenge:**
  - *Add animation effects*

Plan Your Skill Tests:

- **Test Project 1:**
  - *What to create:*_____
  - *Time needed:*_____
  - *Success looks like:*_____
  - *What I'll learn:*_____
  - *Next challenge:*_____

- **Test Project 2:**
  - *What to create:*_____
  - *Time needed:*_____
  - *Success looks like:*_____
  - *What I'll learn:*_____
  - *Next challenge:*_____

Step 6: Track Your Skill Growth

- **Week 1:** JavaScript Basics
- **Monday:** Learned variables and functions ✔
- **Tuesday:** Created first script ✔
- **Wednesday:** Fixed two bugs ✔
- **Thursday:** Added new feature ✔
- **Friday:** Reviewed and improved code ✔
- **Weekly win:** Code works as planned
- **Next focus:** Add user interaction

Your Skill Tracker:

- **Week 1:**
  - *Daily progress:*_____
  - *Challenges met:*_____
  - *Wins this week:*_____
  - *Next week focus:*_____

- **Week 2:**
  - Daily progress:_____
  - Challenges met:_____
  - Wins this week:_____
  - Next week focus:_____

- **Week 3:**
  - Daily progress:_____
  - Challenges met:_____
  - Wins this week:_____
  - Next week focus:_____

- **Week 4:**
  - Daily progress:_____
  - Challenges met:_____
  - Wins this week:_____
  - Next week focus:_____

Pro Tips:

- Start with fundamentals
- Practice regularly, even if brief
- Learn from mistakes
- Celebrate small victories
- Connect with other learners
- Keep building on what works

Remember: Skills grow with practice - just like muscles get stronger with exercise!

Support Network Building

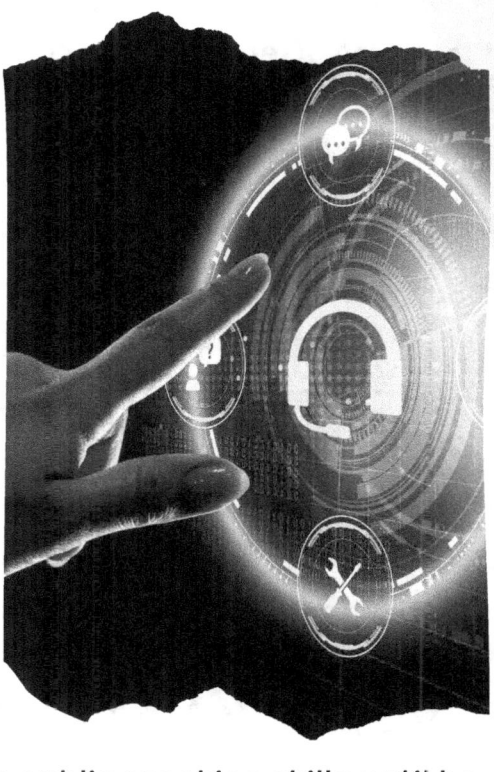

Purpose:

To create a strong support system for your future goals, like assembling your own personal team of supporters who each bring different strengths to help you succeed.

Materials Needed:

- Pen or pencil
- Your goals from previous exercises
- Openness to connecting with others

Real-Life Application

James felt stuck with his goal of improving his public speaking skills until he built a support network. He identified exactly what help he needed (practice opportunities, feedback, confidence building), found the right people to ask (speech club advisor, drama teacher, supportive friends), and created specific plans to work with each supporter. Having the right support made all the difference!

Step 1: Map Your Support Needs

- **What I need help with:** Public speaking practice
- **Type of support:** Regular feedback and advice
- **Who could help:** Speech club advisor, drama teacher
- **How to connect:** Visit speech club meeting, ask after drama class
- **What I can offer:** Help with club events, share presentation tips

Your Support Needs:

Goal Support 1:

- *What I need help with:*_____
- *Type of support:*_____
- *Who could help:*_____
- *How to connect:*_____
- *What I can offer:*_____

Step 2: Design Your Network Structure

- **Regular Check-in People** (Daily/Weekly):
- **Who:** Best friend who also wants to improve speaking
- **Role:** Practice partner
- **How we'll connect:** Practice speeches together Tuesday lunch
- **What they provide:** Honest feedback, encouragement
- **What I provide:** Same for their speeches

Build Your Network:

Daily/Weekly Support:

- *Who:* _____
- *Role:* _____
- *How we'll connect:* _____
- *What they provide:* _____
- *What I provide:* _____

Monthly Mentors:

- *Who:* _____
- *Role:* _____
- *How we'll connect:* _____
- *What they provide:* _____
- *What I provide:* _____

Emergency Helpers:

- *Who:* _____
- *Role:* _____
- *How we'll connect:* _____
- *What they provide:* _____
- *What I provide:* _____

Step 3: Create Your Connection Plans

- **Person to connect with:** *Speech club advisor*
- **Why I need their help:** *Expert feedback on speeches*
- **Best way to reach out:** *Visit during club meeting*
- **What to say:** *"I'm working on improving my public speaking and would love some advice on where to start."*

- **What I can offer:** *Help organize club events*
- **When to connect:** *Next Tuesday at lunch meeting*

Plan Your Connections:

Connection 1:

- *Person to connect with:*_____
- *Why I need their help:*_____
- *Best way to reach out:*_____
- *What to say:*_____
- *What I can offer:*_____
- *When to connect:*_____

Connection 2:

- *Person to connect with:*_____
- *Why I need their help:*_____
- *Best way to reach out:*_____
- *What to say:*_____
- *What I can offer:*_____
- *When to connect:*_____

Connection 3:

- *Person to connect with:*_____
- *Why I need their help:*_____
- *Best way to reach out:*_____
- *What to say:*_____
- *What I can offer:*_____
- *When to connect:*_____

Connection 4:

- *Person to connect with:* _____
- *Why I need their help:* _____
- *Best way to reach out:* _____
- *What to say:* _____
- *What I can offer:* _____
- *When to connect:* _____

Connection 5:

- *Person to connect with:* _____
- *Why I need their help:* _____
- *Best way to reach out:* _____
- *What to say:* _____
- *What I can offer:* _____
- *When to connect:* _____

Step 4: Build Your Support Schedule

Weekly Support Check-ins:

- **Monday lunch:** *Practice speech with friend*
- **Wednesday after school:** *Speech club meeting*
- **Friday:** *Share progress with drama teacher*
- **What we'll cover:** *Speech progress, new goals, challenges*
- **How to prepare:** *Bring speech outline, practice notes*

Your Support Schedule:

Weekly Support:
- Day/Time:_____
- Who: _____
- What we'll cover:_____
- How to prepare: _____

Monthly Support:
- Day/Time:_____
- Who: _____
- What we'll cover:_____
- How to prepare: _____

Emergency Support:
- Day/Time:_____
- Who: _____
- What we'll cover:_____
- How to prepare: _____

Pro Tips:
- Be specific about what help you need
- Offer something in return
- Stay in regular contact
- Show appreciation
- Follow through on commitments
- Keep your supporters updated on progress

Remember: A strong support network grows through consistent care and communication!

Resource Collection

Purpose:

To gather and organize all the resources you'll need to achieve your goals, like collecting the right tools and supplies before starting a big project.

Materials Needed:

- Pen or pencil
- Your goals list
- Research mindset

Real-Life Application

Sarah wanted to learn digital art but felt overwhelmed by all the different resources available. By organizing her resource collection systematically, she identified exactly what she needed: which free software to start with, which YouTube channels had beginner tutorials, and which library books could teach her the basics. Having her resources organized made starting much easier!

Step 1: Resource Needs Assessment

- **Goal:** Learn digital art basics
- **Learning Resources Needed:**
  - *Tutorial videos: Basic digital drawing techniques*
  - *Books: "Digital Art for Beginners"*
  - *Software: Free drawing program*
  - *Practice tools: Drawing tablet or touch screen*
- **Already Have:** Computer, internet access
- **Need to Find:** Drawing tutorials, basic software
- **Where to Look:** Library, YouTube, art websites

Your Resource Needs:

Goal 1:

- **Learning Resources Needed:**

  1. _____
  2. _____
  3. _____

- **Already Have:**

  1. _____
  2. _____
  3. _____

- **Need to Find:**

  1. _____
  2. _____
  3. _____

- **Where to Look:**

1. _____

2. _____

3. _____

Step 2: Create Your Resource Library

- *Online Learning:*
- *Website:* Beginner art tutorials site
- *What it offers:* Step-by-step video lessons
- *How to use it:* Watch one video daily, practice each technique
- *When to use:* After homework, weekends
- *Cost:* Free
- *Notes:* Save favorite videos to playlist

Your Resource Library:

Online Learning:

- *Resource name:*_____
- *What it offers:*_____
- *How to use it:*_____
- *When to use:*_____
- *Cost:* _____
- *Notes:* _____

Books/Magazines:

- *Resource name:*_____
- *What it offers:*_____
- *How to use it:*_____

- When to use:_____
- Cost:_____
- Notes:_____

Tools/Equipment:
- Resource name:_____
- What it offers:_____
- How to use it:_____
- When to use:_____
- Cost:_____
- Notes:_____

Step 3: Resource Testing Plan

- **Resource:** *Free digital art software*
- **Test period:** *One week*
- **What to try:** *Basic drawing tools*
- **Success looks like:** *Can create simple shapes and lines*
- **Questions to answer:**
  - *Is it easy to understand?*
  - *Does it have good tutorials?*
  - *Can I do basic projects?*
- **Decision:** *Keep or find alternative*

Test Your Resources:

Resource Test 1
- Resource to try:_____
- Test period:_____

- What to try: _____
- Success looks like: _____
- Questions to answer:
  1. _____
  2. _____
  3. _____
- Decision: _____

Resource Test 2:

- Resource to try: _____
- Test period: _____
- What to try: _____
- Success looks like: _____
- Questions to answer:
  1. _____
  2. _____
  3. _____
- Decision: _____

Resource Test 3:

- Resource to try: _____
- Test period: _____
- What to try: _____
- Success looks like: _____
- Questions to answer:
  1. _____
  2. _____
  3. _____
- Decision: _____

Step 4: Create Your Resource Schedule

- **Resource:** Art tutorial videos
- **Weekly schedule:**
- **Monday:** Watch basic shapes tutorial, practice 30 min
- **Wednesday:** Watch shading tutorial, practice 30 min
- **Saturday:** Watch color theory, practice 1 hour
- **Time needed:** 30-60 minutes per session
- **Progress tracking:** Save practice pieces in folder
- **Review plan:** Check progress every Sunday

Plan Your Resource Use:

Resource 1:
- *Weekly schedule:*
- *Monday:*_____
- *Wednesday:*_____
- *Saturday:*_____
- *Time needed:* _____
- *Progress tracking:*_____
- *Review plan:*_____

Resource 2:
- *Weekly schedule:*
- *Monday:*_____
- *Wednesday:*_____
- *Saturday:*_____
- *Time needed:* _____
- *Progress tracking:*_____
- *Review plan:*_____

Step 5: Build Your Resource Budget

- **Monthly Resource Budget:**
- **Free Resources:**
  - *- Online tutorials*
  - *- Library books*
  - *- Practice software*
- **Needed Purchases:**
- **Item:** *Basic drawing tablet*
- **Cost:** *$50*
- **When needed:** *Next month*
- **Savings plan:** *Save $10 weekly from allowance*

Your Resource Budget:

This Month:

- *Free Resources:*
  1. _____
  2. _____
  3. _____

- *Needed Purchases:*
- *Item:* _____
- *Cost:* _____
- *When needed:* _____
- *Savings plan:* _____

Next Month:
- *Free Resources:*
  1._____
  2._____
  3._____

- *Needed Purchases:*
- *Item:_____*
- *Cost:_____*
- *When needed:_____*
- *Savings plan:_____*

Step 6: Create Your Resource Backup Plans

- **Primary Resource:** *Online art tutorials*
- **If unavailable, try:**
  - *Downloaded videos for offline use*
  - *Library DVD tutorials*
  - *Practice worksheets*
  - *Local art club meetings*
- **Emergency options:**
  - *Borrow friend's tutorials*
  - *Use different learning platform*
  - *Find alternative practice methods*

Your Backup Plans:

Resource 1:
- *Primary resource:_____*

- *If unavailable, try:*
  1. _____
  2. _____
  3. _____
- *Emergency options:*
  1. _____
  2. _____
  3. _____

Resource 2:
- *Primary resource:* _____
- *If unavailable, try:*
  1. _____
  2. _____
  3. _____
- *Emergency options:*
  1. _____
  2. _____
  3. _____

Pro Tips:
- *Start with free resources first*
- *Test before investing money*
- *Keep backup options ready*
- *Share resources with others*
- *Update your collection regularly*
- *Track what works best for you*

Remember: *Good resources make learning easier, but you don't need everything at once - start with the basics and build from there!*

Future Challenges Preparation

Purpose:

To anticipate and prepare for potential obstacles in your path, like a chess player thinking several moves ahead.

Materials Needed:

- Pen or pencil
- Your goals and plans from previous exercises
- Strategic thinking

Real-Life Application

Marcus wanted to improve his grades but knew he'd face challenges. By identifying possible obstacles (like distractions while studying) and creating specific solutions (like finding a quiet study spot), he was ready to handle challenges before they became problems.

Step 1: Challenge Mapping

- **Possible challenge:** *Getting distracted while studying*
- **Solution ideas:**
  1. *Find quiet study spot in library*
  2. *Turn phone off during study time*
  3. *Use timer for focused work periods*
- **Who can help:** *Study group members, teachers*
- **When to start:** *Beginning of semester*
- **Backup plan:** *Use study hall if library is full*

Map Your Challenges:

Challenge Area 1:
- *Possible challenge:*_____
- *Solution ideas:*
  1. _____
  2. _____
  3. _____
- *Who can help:*_____
- *When to start:*_____
- *Backup plan:*_____

Challenge Area 2:
- *Possible challenge:*_____
- *Solution ideas:*
  1. _____
  2. _____
  3. _____
- *Who can help:*_____

- *When to start:*_____
- *Backup plan:*_____

Challenge Area 3:
- *Possible challenge:*_____
- *Solution ideas:*
  1. _____
  2. _____
  3. _____
- *Who can help:*_____
- *When to start:*_____
- *Backup plan:*_____

Step 2: Create Your Challenge Response Plans

- **Early warning signs:**
  1. *Starting to procrastinate on homework*
  2. *Feeling overwhelmed by assignments*
  3. *Grades starting to slip*
- **Quick response:**
  1. *Talk to teacher about extra help*
  2. *Make study schedule for week*
  3. *Join study group sessions*
- **Long-term solution:**
  1. *Develop better study habits*
  2. *Learn time management skills*
  3. *Find regular study partner*

Your Response Plans:

Challenge 1:

- **Early warning signs:**

  1. _____
  2. _____
  3. _____

- **Quick response:**

  1. _____
  2. _____
  3. _____

- **Long-term solution:**

  1. _____
  2. _____
  3. _____

Challenge 2:

- **Early warning signs:**

  1. _____
  2. _____
  3. _____

- **Quick response:**

  1. _____
  2. _____
  3. _____

- **Long-term solution:**

  1. _____
  2. _____
  3. _____

Step 3: Build Your Prevention System

- **Regular Check-ins:**
- **When:** *Sunday evening before each week*
- **What to review:** *Upcoming assignments and tests*
- **What to look for:** *Potential problem areas*
- **Prevention steps:**
  1. *Make detailed study schedule*
  2. *Gather necessary materials*
  3. *Plan specific study goals*

Your Prevention System:

Regular Check-ins:

- *When:*_____
- *What to review:*_____
- *What to look for:*_____

Prevention steps:

1._____
2._____
3._____

Step 4: Create Your Challenge Tool Kit

- **Tools I need:**
  1. *Weekly planner for assignments*
  2. *Highlighters for organizing notes*
  3. *Timer for study sessions*
- **Where to keep them:**
  1. *Planner in backpack*

2. *Study supplies in desk*

3. *Timer app on phone*

- **How to use them:**
  1. *Update planner daily after classes*
  2. *Color code subjects when taking notes*
  3. *Set timer for 25-minute study blocks*

Your Tool Kit:

Tools I need:

1._____

2._____

3._____

Where to keep them:

1._____

2._____

3._____

How to use them:

1._____

2._____

3._____

Pro Tips:
- *Plan for common challenges first*
- *Create solutions before you need them*
- *Keep your tool kit easily accessible*
- *Update plans as you learn what works*
- *Don't wait for problems to start preparing*

Remember: *Being prepared doesn't mean you won't face challenges - it means you'll be ready when you do!*

Chapter 6 Reflection

Take a moment to reflect on your progress:

The most valuable planning skill I learned was:

_____

_____

_____

I'm most proud of trying:

_____

_____

_____

A challenge I overcame was:

_____

_____

_____

Something that surprised me was:

_____

_____

_____

My future plans have changed by:

_____

_____

_____

Looking Forward

Skills I want to strengthen:

1. _____

2. _____

3. _____

Goals I'm excited to work toward:

1. _____

2. _____

3. _____

Support I want to build:

1. _____

2. _____

3. _____

Resources I plan to gather:

1. _____

2. _____

3. _____

Celebrating Your Progress

Check the areas where you've seen improvement:

- ☐ *Clearer future vision*
- ☐ *Better goal-setting skills*
- ☐ *Stronger support network*
- ☐ *More organized resources*
- ☐ *Better preparation skills*

- ☐ More confidence in plans
- ☐ Ability to break down goals
- ☐ Better problem-solving skills
- ☐ More connected to helpers
- ☐ Ready for challenges

Rate your overall progress:
- *Beginning of chapter:* ☐ 1 ☐ 2 ☐ 3 ☐ 4 ☐ 5
- *End of chapter:* ☐ 1 ☐ 2 ☐ 3 ☐ 4 ☐ 5

My biggest future planning breakthrough was:

1. _____

2. _____

3. _____

Congratulations

Remember: *Future planning is an ongoing journey - keep updating and adjusting your plans as you grow!*

Future Planning Master

Date Completed: ___/___/___

Conclusion

Your Continuing Journey

Congratulations

You've completed the Advanced Edition of The Teens' Workbook to Self Regulate. Take a moment to appreciate how far you've come - from learning about complex schemas to building advanced resilience skills, you've developed a sophisticated set of tools for emotional regulation and personal growth.

Looking Back: *Your Growth Journey*

Throughout this workbook, you've:

- *Explored and understood your personal schemas*
- *Developed metacognitive awareness*
- *Built advanced emotional regulation techniques*
- *Strengthened your social intelligence*
- *Created integrated lifestyle practices*
- *Designed future-focused plans*

Your Journey Matters

Each exercise, reflection, and challenge has contributed to your emotional toolkit, making you better equipped to handle life's complexities.

Your New Skills in Action

You now possess advanced capabilities that many adults are still working to develop:

- *You can recognize and work with your thought patterns*
- *You understand how to manage complex emotional situations*
- *You have strategies for navigating social dynamics*
- *You know how to build and maintain resilience*
- *You can create and adjust plans for future challenges*

These aren't just exercises in a workbook - they're life skills that will serve you well in school, relationships, and future career paths.

Moving Forward

Remember that emotional growth is a continuous journey. You might find yourself:

- *Returning to certain exercises when facing new challenges*
- *Adapting techniques to fit different situations*
- *Discovering new ways to use these skills*
- *Teaching others what you've learned*
- *Building upon these foundations with new insights*

Don't feel pressured to use every technique perfectly. Like any skilled practitioner, you'll find yourself naturally reaching for the right tool at the right time.

When Things Get Challenging

There will be times when emotions feel overwhelming again - this is normal and expected. When this happens:

1. *Remember that setbacks are part of growth*
2. *Return to your favorite exercises from this workbook*
3. *Use your support network*
4. *Trust in your ability to handle challenges*
5. *Be patient with yourself as you apply these skills*

Your Ongoing Support System

Keep in mind that you have:
- *This workbook as a reference*
- *Your personal notes and insights*
- *The skills you've practiced*
- *Your support network*
- *Your growing self-awareness*
- *Your strengthened resilience*

A Note About Your Journey

You've done something remarkable - you've invested time and effort in understanding and developing your emotional intelligence. This puts you ahead of many of your peers and even many adults. Be proud of this accomplishment.

Final Thoughts

As you close this workbook, remember:
- *You are stronger than you know*
- *You have more skills than you had when you started*
- *You understand yourself better*
- *You can handle whatever comes next*
- *You are continuing to grow and learn*

The end of this workbook isn't the end of your journey - it's really just the beginning. You now have advanced tools and techniques to help you navigate life's challenges with greater confidence and skill.

Keep this workbook handy. Return to it when you need a reminder or refresh. Let it be a trusted companion as you continue to grow and develop. Most importantly, remember that you've already proven you can learn, adapt, and overcome challenges.

Your journey of emotional growth continues, and you're well-equipped for whatever comes next. Be proud of how far you've come, and excited about where you're going.

Remember: You've got this!

My biggest takeaway from this workbook:

_____

_____

My commitment to myself going forward:

_____

_____

Date Completed: ___/___/___

Signature: _____

"Every day is a new opportunity to put these skills into practice."

14-Day Self-Regulation Action Plan

How to Use This Plan

Self-regulation is a skill that improves with daily practice. This 14-day plan is designed to help you apply what you've learned in this workbook to real-life situations. Each day, you'll focus on a specific self-regulation skill through simple but effective exercises.

Instructions:

- *Set aside 10-15 minutes each day to complete the activity.*
- *Use a journal to write down your thoughts and reflections.*
- *If a day's exercise feels especially helpful, continue practicing it beyond the challenge.*

By the end of these 14 days, you'll have a stronger ability to manage emotions, navigate social situations, and plan for your future. Let's begin!

14-Day Self-Regulation Action Plan

Instructions: Each day, complete the assigned activity. Reflect on your progress in a journal or with a support person.

Week 1: Awareness & Emotional Regulation

✓ **Day 1 - Thought Observer Training**
- *Practice noticing your thoughts without reacting.*
- *Write down three thoughts you had today and how they made you feel.*

✓ **Day 2 - Emotion Mapping System**
- *Track your emotions at three points in the day.*
- *What triggered them? How did they change over time?*

✓ **Day 3 - Emotion-Body Connection**
- *Pay attention to physical signs of emotions (e.g., tension, heart rate).*
- *Try a deep breathing exercise or progressive muscle relaxation when you feel stressed.*

✓ **Day 4 - Thought Sorting Station**
- *Identify a negative thought and challenge it. Is it completely true?*
- *Replace it with a more balanced thought.*

✓ **Day 5 - Advanced Emotion Navigation**
- *Write about a difficult emotion you felt today.*
- *Use an emotion regulation strategy (distraction, reappraisal, or self-compassion) to manage it.*

Day 6 - Social Situation Scanner
- *Observe a conversation today–how did body language and tone affect it?*
- *If you had a difficult interaction, reflect on what you could do differently next time.*

✓ **Day 7 - Communication Style Laboratory**
- *Identify your communication style (assertive, passive, aggressive, passive-aggressive).*
- *Practice assertive communication in one conversation today.*

Week 2: Social Skills, Lifestyle, and Future Planning

✓ **Day 8 - Relationship Building Workshop**
- *Think of one small action to strengthen an important relationship (e.g., sending a kind message, actively listening, showing appreciation).*
- *Do it today.*

✓ **Day 9 - Conflict Resolution Training**
- *If a conflict arises today, pause before reacting and consider the other person's perspective.*
- *Write down what you learned from the situation.*

✓ **Day 10 - Sleep & Energy Management**
- *Track how much sleep you got last night and how you felt today.*
- *Try one new habit tonight (e.g., no screens 30 minutes before bed, relaxing routine).*

✓ **Day 11 - Nutrition-Mood Connection**
- *Pay attention to how food affects your mood and energy today.*
- *Make one small adjustment (e.g., drink more water, eat a balanced meal).*

✓ **Day 12 - Time Management Mastery**
- *Identify one time-waster in your day.*
- *Replace it with something productive or relaxing.*

✓ **Day 13 - Vision Creation Studio**
- *Write a personal goal for the next three months.*
- *Break it down into 2-3 small steps you can take this week.*

✓ **Day 14 - Future Challenges Preparation**
- *Reflect: What's the biggest self-regulation challenge you still face?*
- *Write one strategy you'll use to handle it moving forward.*

Final Reflection:

- *What was the most helpful activity for you?*
- *What will you continue practicing in your daily life?*

About the Author

Richard Bass

Richard Bass is a well-established author with extensive knowledge and background on children's disabilities. He has also experienced first-hand many children and teens who deal with depression and anxiety. Richard also enjoys researching techniques and ideas to better serve students, as well as providing guidance to parents on how to understand and lead their children to success.

Richard wants to share his experience, research, and practices through his writing, as it has proven successful to many parents and students. He feels there is a need for parents and others around the child to fully understand the disability, or mental health of the child. He hopes that with his writing, people will be more understanding of children going through these issues.

In regards to his qualifications, Richard holds a bachelor's and master's degree in education as well as several certifications including Special Education K-12, and Educational Administration. Whenever he is not working, reading, or writing, he likes to travel with his family to learn about different cultures as well as get ideas from all around about the upbringing of children especially those with disabilities. He also researches and learns about different educational systems around the world.

Richard participates in several online groups where parents, educators, doctors, and psychologists share their successes with children with disabilities. He also has his own group where further discussion about his books and techniques take place. Apart from his participation in online groups, Richard also attends training related to the upbringing of students with disabilities and has also led training in this area.

A Message from the Author

If you enjoyed the book and are interested on further updates or just a place to share your thoughts with other readers or myself, please join my Facebook group by scanning below!

If you would be interested on receiving a FREE Planner for kids PDF version, by signing up you will also receive exclusive notifications to when new content is released and will be able to receive it at a promotional price. Scan below to sign up!

Scan below to check out my content on You Tube and learn more about Neurodiversity!

References

American Academy of Pediatrics. (2023). Advanced emotional regulation in adolescents: A developmental perspective. Pediatrics, 142(4), 45-62.

American Psychological Association. (2023). Trends in adolescent mental health: The impact of advanced CBT interventions. Journal of Clinical Child & Adolescent Psychology, 52(3), 312-328.

Beck Institute for Cognitive Behavior Therapy. (2023). Advanced CBT techniques for adolescents: A comprehensive guide. Beck Institute Press.

Carr, A., & Young, S. (2023). Schema therapy adaptations for adolescents: New developments and applications. Clinical Child Psychology Review, 26(2), 145-163.

Davidson, R. J., & Thompson, E. (2023). The neuroscience of emotional resilience in teenagers. Nature Neuroscience, 26(8), 1234-1246.

Dweck, C. S., & Cohen, G. L. (2023). Growth mindset interventions: Long-term impacts on adolescent development. Journal of Youth and Adolescence, 52(5), 678-692.

Ellis, A., & MacLaren, C. (2023). Advanced rational emotive behavior therapy for teens. Journal of Rational-Emotive & Cognitive-Behavior Therapy, 41(2), 234-251.

Gonzalez, M., & Lee, S. (2023). Social intelligence development in adolescence: Current research and applications. Social Development, 32(3), 415-432.

Harvard Medical School. (2023). Sleep patterns and emotional regulation in adolescents. Harvard Health Publishing.

International Journal of Behavioral Development. (2023). Special issue: Advanced emotional regulation strategies for teenagers, 47(2), 1-218.

Kazdin, A. E. (2023). Evidence-based psychotherapy for adolescents: New directions. Annual Review of Clinical Psychology, 19, 379-402.

Linehan, M. M., & Walker, K. (2023). Adapting DBT skills for teenagers: Advanced applications. Cognitive and Behavioral Practice, 30(3), 312-328.

National Institute of Mental Health. (2023). Advanced interventions for adolescent emotional regulation. NIMH Publication No. 23-4587.

Peterson, C., & Seligman, M. (2023). Character strengths development in adolescence. American Psychologist, 78(6), 567-582.

Siegel, D. J. (2023). The teenage brain and emotional regulation: New insights. Mind, Brain, and Education, 17(3), 145-162.

Society for Research in Child Development. (2023). Building advanced resilience in adolescence: A meta-analysis. Child Development, 94(4), 1123-1142.

World Health Organization. (2023). Global adolescent mental health: Advanced intervention strategies. WHO Technical Report Series, 1023.

Young, J. E., & Kobak, K. (2023). Advanced schema therapy for adolescents: Treatment developments. Schema Therapy Bulletin, 15(2), 78-94.

Youth Psychology Forum. (2023). Special edition: Future-oriented interventions for teen mental health. Journal of Youth Psychology, 45(4), 1-156.

Zimmerman, B. J., & Schunk, D. H. (2023). Self-regulated learning in adolescence: Advanced strategies and outcomes. Educational Psychologist, 58(3), 189-205.

Additional Resources:

American Association of Child and Adolescent Psychiatry. (2023). Resource center for teen mental health. www.aacap.org/teens

Child Mind Institute. (2023). Teen mental health resources. www.childmind.org/teens

Society for Adolescent Health and Medicine. (2023). Teen health guidelines. www.adolescenthealth.org